COMPUTERS

FOR BEGINNERS

ERROL SELKIRK

ILLUSTRATED BY BENNY KANDLER

Writers and Readers

WRITERS AND READERS PUBLISHING, INC.
P.O. Box 461, Village Station
New York, NY 10014

c/o Airlift Book Company
26 Eden Grove
London N78EF
England

•

ISBN # 0-86316-91-X
2 3 4 5 6 7 8 9 0

Manufactured in the United States of America

Beginners Documentary Comic Books are published by Writers and
Readers Publishing Inc. Its trademark, consisting of the words "For
Beginners, Writers and Readers Documentary Comic Books" and the
Writers and Readers logo, is registered in the U.S. Patent and Trademark
Office and in other countries.

About the Author

Errol Selkirk has had a lifelong interest in the sciences dating back to the launching of Sputnik in 1957. After studying philosophy in college, he worked as a journalist and then as a writer of educational texts and science articles. His first experience with computers came when he created the learning software for a children's computer program. Now an editor, he lives in New York with a wife, child, and electronic typewriter.

About the Illustrator

Benny Kandler is a cartoonist, illustrator and graphic designer whose works have been published in Czechoslovakia, Germany and Britain. He draws a regular cartoon strip for *Practical Wireless*. He lives in Cambridge (UK) with a wife, pussycat and an old mechanical typewriter.

Chapter I
INTRODUCTION

"Make things as simple as possible.
But no simpler."
　　　　　– Albert Einstein

Computers are not only changing the world.
They are also changing the way we
think about the world
and our place within it.

If this statement seems a trifle broad, a quick look around will show
the many ways that it is true. Not that computers are about to abolish
gravity or make hunger instantly disappear. Yet the effects of this
new technology are certainly profound and far-reaching, as can
easily be seen...

In the automated offices and factories where we work. Or where some of us used to work before the coming of computers and industrial robots.

In the way that business does business. And in the way that governments govern.

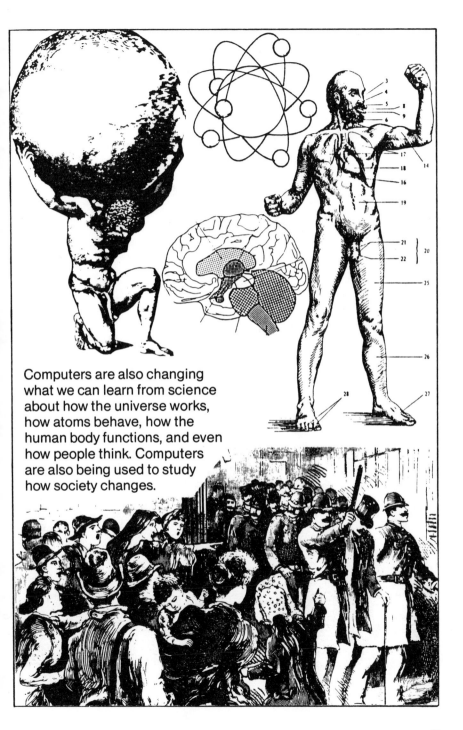

Computers are also changing
what we can learn from science
about how the universe works,
how atoms behave, how the
human body functions, and even
how people think. Computers
are also being used to study
how society changes.

3

Some of the changes around us may seem trivial. Video games and computerized coffee pots – how could I ever have survived without it?

But many other of these changes are of critical importance. Some hold out the promise of a better world to all of us. Some changes will only benefit those who own and control the machines or have access to them.

What, after all, is a computer? Is it just a souped-up adding machine? A mechanical super brain? A dream machine to grant all our wishes? Or a doomsday device that will put an end to our wishing once and for all?

Essentially, the computer is a tool, an extension of the human mind and body – possibly the most important technical development since fire. Computers extend the mind's ability to observe the world and ourselves, and make sense of what we see. And by linking this tool to other machines, we are better able to predict and even control events happening around us.

Throughout history, people have sought just such a tool through science or magic. A thirteenth-century inventor, Ramon Lüll, is said to have actually constructed a peculiar computational device called Ars Magna. This machine is supposed to have been able to manipulate symbols to make predictions, based on a theoretical system that linked logic, astrology, and tarot. Unfortunately, we have no idea how this amazing tool worked – since it was destroyed as the Devil's Work.

Today we describe what computers do and how they do it in terms of science. But like the sorcerer's machine, today's computers manipulate information about what was and what is in order to get a better grasp on what will be.

The basis of the computer's power is its amazing ability to handle numbers and facts -- data -- at speeds far faster than any human or group of humans. A computer in a bank, for example, can scan information on checks 10,000 times faster than even the quickest clerk. And today's new generation of super computers can multiply hundreds of millions of numbers in a single second.

Try that on your pocket calculator.

Information has always had value. Without good information it's difficult if not impossible to make intelligent decisions. In the past, farmers consulted almanacs that attempted to predict when the last freeze of the season would occur, and when it was safe to plant their crops. This essential information was traditionally pieced together by examining past weather patterns and certain natural signs such as the appearance of the ground hog or the thickness of animal fur and tree bark. This data was thought to indicate future weather trends.

Modern computers are capable of taking in great masses of raw data, and finding certain weather patterns which may point to one trend or the other. The computers are even able to state how certain or uncertain their predictions are, based upon the amount of information available and its value. The system used by the US Weather Service processes billions of bits of data annually.

Farmers then use this information – coupled with their own knowledge of local conditions and the various needs of specific plants – to decide which crops to plant and when.

Computers supply this kind of *decision support* in nearly every area of modern life.

From the Air Force general who needs good information – what they call intelligence – about a possible enemy radar center in the Arctic...

Military intelligence is a contradiction in terms.

Groucho Marx

To a shopkeeper who needs to know how many widgets are still in her warehouse, in order to decide if she needs to order any more.

Yet information has value only to those who can learn from it and use it.

US MADE

WIDGETS

US MADE

WIDGET

DATA: A large cargo ship was spotted off the southern coast at 6 o'clock.

For the casual hiker who spotted the big vessel on the horizon, this fact was simply a novel addition to the sunset. It has no other meaning unless the hiker shares the data with someone else, say, a coast guard officer, who uses his own knowledge to interpret the data.

INFORMATION: Judging from the shape of the ship, its size, markings, and speed – it seems to match the description of a cargo vessel, The Neptune, which we expect any day.

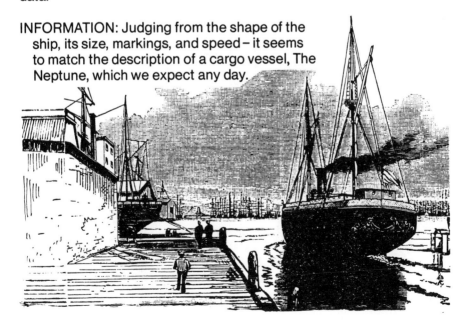

11

This information may simply be rendered as a couple lines in the officer's log. It has no other meaning unless he's been instructed to send a message to the capital with the news. There, the information can have many meanings. To the port officials, it might mean that they'd better get the piers ready. To the dockworkers it might mean a couple weeks worth of work unloading cargo. And to the businesspeople of the port, this information will force them to make use of their knowledge of local supply and demand to make important decisions.

APPLICATION: The Neptune is expected to carry six months supply of bananas. This is likely to drive prices down. So a smart buyer will know enough to wait until after the ship has docked. But a smart seller will know that she must sell before the cargo comes on the market.

This scenario, incidentally, is similar to the one created by the great scientist, Galileo, who tried to interest the merchants of Venice in his new telescope – one of the earliest information enhancers. Galileo tried with only limited success to make the merchants see the advantage of getting good information in the shortest possible time. The telescope was his solution to the information problem. The computer, linked to a worldwide telecommunications system, is ours today.

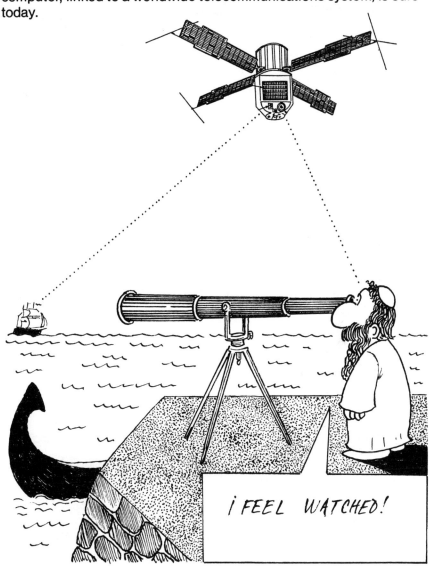

The story of the SS Neptune also illustrates the relationship of data and information to knowledge. You can't have knowledge of something without the facts. But the facts alone don't do you much good without the knowledge of how to interpret and make use of them.

Knowledge is not just the result of processing information. Knowledge is also necessary for setting up the process in the first place. It's what lets us make sense out of details and patterns. We need knowledge to guide the whole process along.

So where do we get knowledge? One of the best ways is to pursue the facts honestly. That requires openness and flexibility. We let the facts touch and even change us. We ask one question, get an answer, let the answer shape our next question, and so on.

And we don't just use the facts to prove what we knew before we started.

"There are three kinds of lies. Lies. Damn lies. And statistics."
– Mark Twain

Finally, honesty requires that sometimes we admit that the assumptions we began with were biased, false, or just simply inadequate. Computer scientists have a word for this: G.I.G.O. Which means garbage in, garbage out.

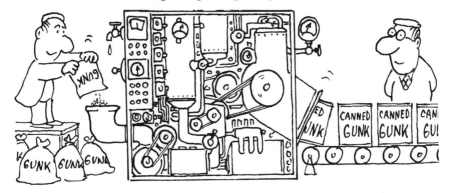

The pursuit of knowledge is an adventure into unknown territory. And as any traveller will swear, you really can't know another place unless you've actually been there, met its people, smelled its smells, felt its weather on your skin, experienced the scale and pace of the place in your own life.

Computers too are something to be experienced directly. With a language, logic, pace, and feel of their own. Experienced computer users have learned their machines' capacities and limitations. They've interacted, *interfaced*. They know how to "think" computer. The rest of us only think about them.

No single book can give you total knowledge about computers, how to use them, or how they're changing the world. The best anyone can do is to give the reader an informed framework in which to pursue his or her own exploration.

If you know little or nothing about computer technology, this might be the kind of introduction you need to get personally more involved.

If you're already knowledgeable in the subject, questions raised in this book may help you evaluate your own experience with computers in the light of past developments, current uses, and possible futures.

In either case, probably the best way to get to know your way around this rapidly changing science is simply to...

Chapter II
NUMBERS, NEEDS & INNOVATIONS

"Be fruitful and multiply."
— The Bible

A primitive form of human being may have walked the earth three million years ago. From that time until roughly 10,000 years ago, people had little or no need for thinking tools like computers to help them count or calculate.

Our species lived in small, compact bands that survived by hunting and gathering the wild plants and small animals that came their way. Probably all the numbers they needed were "one" and "many".

Life began to get more complex sometime after the last Ice Age. People seemed to have a need to keep track of bigger numbers. A primitive counter from that time, made from the jawbone of a wolf, was recently found in Czechoslovakia. It had 55 marks in it, arranged in groups of five.

Ordering things in terms of five and ten was no accident, considering that our species has five fingers on each of two hands.

The numerical system most of us use today is still based on 10 – the decimal system. Deci is Latin for the number 10.

For simple counting, the fingers on a person's hands were usually satisfactory. In a pinch, a person could also use her toes or those of a neighbor. This 20-based system can still be seen in the French word for 80 – quatre-vingt – meaning four twenties. The number twenty is also the basis for the English word "score", as in Lincoln's Gettysburg Address:

Four score and seven years ago ...

$$20 + 20 + 20 + 20 + 7$$

Which had much more poetry in it than plain old 87. Another vestige of this number system was the old 20-shilling British pound.

The development of agriculture and the domestication of animals both occured about 10,000 years ago. Suddenly there were plenty of things to count. Settlements became towns, and then cities. Architecture, complex economies, governments and religions quickly evolved along the banks of great rivers such as the Nile, Euphrates, Indus, and Yang Tse.

WITH AS MANY CATTLE AS GRAINS OF SAND IN THE DESERT YOU DON'T QUALIFY FOR TAX RELIEF!

Calendars were needed to coordinate the growing cycle and important holy days with the changing seasons and the shifting stars. Rulers needed to count the heads of their subjects and the property they owned for the purpose of taxation. Generals needed to appraise their own military forces and those of the enemy.

And merchants also needed ways of keeping track of their growing accounts.

To deal with large numbers, the ancient Egyptians created a peculiar numerical system represented by hieroglyphic pictures: 10 was a U or a circle; 100 was a coiled rope; 1000 was a lotus blossom; 10,000 was a pointed finger; 100,000 was a tadpole; and 1,000,000 was a picture of a man stretching his arms to heaven in amazement.

And for good reason. Anything that big simply boggled the ancient mind. But things were still pretty confusing with smaller figures. After all, how do you go about multiplying three tadpoles and a lotus by a pointed finger and a circle?

To use these unwieldy numbers, a high caste of mathematical scientists was created. They were the ones who designed the awesome Pyramids, surveyed the fields, and divided up the rich harvest.

OF COURSE, THEY ALSO DID PHARAOH'S TAXES!

These elite scribes also developed the sophisticated 365 day planting calendar used by the Egyptians. It was timed to the rising of the star Sirius in the heavens, the signal for the annual flooding of the fertile Nile.

In Babylon counting took a different direction, based on the number 60. This is the source of our 60 second minute, 60 minute hour, as well as the way we divide a circle into 360 degrees.

A Babylonian clay tablet from around the year 2000 BC contains a list of numbers and their *squares* – a number multiplied by itself – from 1 all the way to 24. This list was apparently used as a reference table for tough geometric problems.

But whoever calculated these squares probably used some kind of mechanical assistance. Most likely a primitive form of the first real computer...

The ABACUS. The invention is Babylonian, but the name is derived from the neighboring Phoenicians, who called a flat slab covered with sand on which figures are drawn, *abak*.

Early abacuses used this board with pebbles placed on lines in the sand. Herodotus, the fifth-century Greek historian, mentioned the pebble abacus and how it was used to calculate the interest on a very large loan:

766 talents, 1095 drachmas, and 5 obols over 1464 days at a rate of one drachma per day for each 5 talents

By the way, "calculate" comes from the Roman word for pebble.

The Chinese, who are still masters of the abacus, introduced the use of bamboo rods and sliding beads in place of stones. Its operation is simple and elegant.

The rods stood for ones, tens, hundreds, and so on. A cross-bar was added that divided each rod into two zones called "heaven" and "earth". Earth contained 5 beads; heaven only 1. On the first rod, each earth bead had a value of 1 and the heaven bead had a value of 5. On the second rod, each earth bead equalled 10, each heaven bead 50. Clear so far?

$$\begin{aligned} 2 \\ + 5 \\ +10 \\ +10 \\ \hline 27 \end{aligned}$$

When the value of the beads on the first rod exceeds 10, 1 is carried over to the next rod. Here is what 27 would look like:

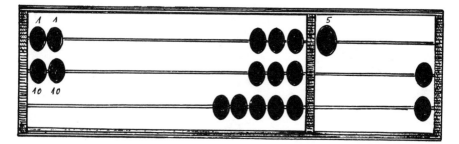

The next great breakthrough took place in neighboring India around 800 AD: the invention of the ZERO. Which was far from nothing. The zero represented the "empty" column on the abacus, when you carry over into the next column.

Now every conceivable number could be represented by a combination of the digits 1–9, plus zero. Also numbers could now be written in a simplified way that mirrored their position on the abacus. 2001, for example, would always mean 2 in the thousands column, zero in the hundreds, zero in the tens, and 1 on the ones.

This fixed positioning made addition, subtraction, multiplication, and division a breeze.

An Arab mathematician called Al-Khowarizmi visited India around 830 AD and learned about both the zero and the decimal system. He wrote an historic book concerning these and other discoveries, *Al-jabr wa'l muqabalah*, which meant "the bringing together of unknowns to match a known quantity", and from which we derived our word algebra. Our system of Arabic numerals, known as algorism, is actually a corruption of the great Al-Khowarizmi's name.

Five centuries later, another Muslim mathematician known as Al-Kashi took the science of calculation even further. He invented a series of mechanical computers which could predict lunar eclipses and other astronomic events.

These clever devices used a pair of sliding metal disks to make calculations – much like the moving rods of a slide rule. To multiply, all you had to do was turn the number on one disk so that it faced a second number on the other disk. A third number – the product – would then miraculously appear.

Europe at this time was a cultural backwater. Awkward Latin numerals were the only counting system available. Just imagine the difficulty involved dividing LXVII by XIV.

Christendom and Islam were also constantly at war. The Arab's new mathematical system was strictly top secret. It took a monk known as Abelard of Bath, who disguised himself as a Muslim and slipped into the University of Cordova, to make this information available to Europeans. Europeans were quick to learn.

Using Arabic numerals and the abacus, European students were expected to solve tough problems such as:

"How many pairs of rabbits will be produced in a year, beginning with a single pair, if in every month each pair bears a new pair which becomes productive from the second month on."

– Positively hare raising! –

England, however, was slow to change. As late as 1636, Bristol city records were still written in Latin numerals. And in London, taxes were being computed on a peculiar table with checkerboard squares. The word Exchequer – the Royal treasury department – comes from that board.

THINK OF SOMETHING SIMPLER, HENRY! A DIVORCE IS AN EXPENSIVE THING NOWADAYS...

Yet some of the most important developments in computer science were to come from the British Isles. The European Renaissance had helped to open minds to the immense possibilities of the natural world. Unfortunately, the need to penetrate these mysteries was hampered by mathematicians' inability to perform complex calculations.

The abacus handled addition and subtraction easily. But multiplication and division were much more problematic. John Napier, a gifted Scotsman, complained of the "slippery errors" and the "tedious amount of time" involved in high level calculation.

So in 1617, Napier invented a multiplying machine made up of a series of movable rods with digits 1 to 9 and their multiples engraved below them. These were known as Napier's Bones. To multiply, you rotated the rods in such a way that the answer could be found by adding numbers in horizontally adjacent areas.

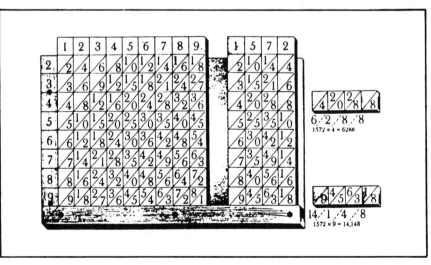

A similar concept was behind the invention of the slide rule, produced by an English clergyman, William Oughtred in 1621. The device had two sliding pieces of wood with numbers and their multiples printed on them. To multiply, you put the number to be multiplied opposite the number 1. Then you look for the multiplier – the number you want the first number multiplied by. Opposite the multiplier is the answer. To divide, you simply reverse the process.

Note that the slide rule, unlike the abacus, does not count anything. It measures a physical property – the length of ruler – that has a certain relationship to a series of numbers. We call this kind of a device an *analog computer* because it deals with calculation on the basis of analogy. The *digital computer*, which actually counts separate numbers, is more precise. Most of today's computers are digital.

Around 1643, Blaise Pascal, a brilliant young French mathematician, invented a mechanical calculator to help his father, a tax collector. It used a series of numbered wheels that automatically carried figures from the ones to the hundreds to the thousands, and so on. In perhaps the first advertisement for a computer ever printed, Pascal wrote:

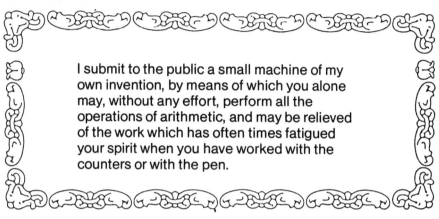

I submit to the public a small machine of my own invention, by means of which you alone may, without any effort, perform all the operations of arithmetic, and may be relieved of the work which has often times fatigued your spirit when you have worked with the counters or with the pen.

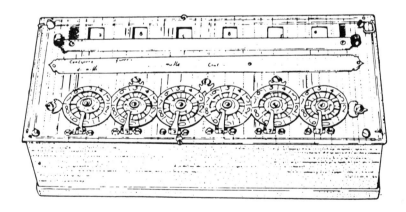

Gottfried Wilhelm von Leibniz, a German Baron active in scientific research of all kinds, also realized that the difficulty of doing calculations was holding back the process of discovery.

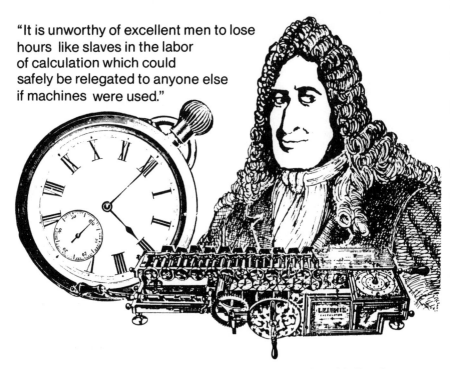

"It is unworthy of excellent men to lose hours like slaves in the labor of calculation which could safely be relegated to anyone else if machines were used."

In 1673, Leibniz constructed his first mechanical multiplier. It worked by turning a wheel, which in turn rotated a series of numbered rods connected by gears. It was the most sophisticated calculator ever invented, and Leibniz felt it was a must for "the managers of financial affairs, the administrators of others' estates, merchants, surveyors, geographers, navigators, astronomers, and those connected with any of the crafts that use mathematics."

Leibniz' basic design, involving numbered rods and gears, was still being used in mechanical calculators built as late as 1970. Advanced beyond its time, the device could still not handle the kinds of involved computation that scientists would soon be needing to bring about the Industrial Revolution.

Spoken like a true child of the Machine Age, and one of the future fathers of computer science. Born in 1791 to an English banking family, Babbage had a lifelong fascination with mechanical devices that perhaps dated back to an exquisite pair of spring-operated metal dancers he marveled at as a boy.

A bright, eccentric student of the sciences, Babbage dedicated himself to modernizing mathematics along the lines set down by Leibniz. Sometime in 1813 he first had the idea of inventing what he called the *analytical engine*, and what we today would call a computer.

"I wish to God these calculations had been executed by steam."
– Charles Babbage

IF WE ONLY HAD A COMPUTER CENTRE!

This was the age in which Britannia truly ruled the waves, with a worldwide empire based upon advanced industrial production at home and naval technology abroad. Yet the further development of all the sciences was still being hampered by the endless labor of calculation – a task normally carried out by caste of skilled clerks called "computers".

Important charts and tables used for navigation, military ballistics, engineering, and insurance simply could not be trusted. Mistakes made in making calculations were further complicated by mistakes made in printing. Government tables for navigation, for example, contained 1100 errors and many pages of corrections.

In 1823 Babbage received a grant from the government to create a mechanical calculator to help deal with ballistics and navigation. This was one of the first official Research and Development grants in history. But it would not be the last to run far over cost and deadline.

A decade later, Babbage's ambitious device was still unfinished. He'd run out of R & D money long before. Now he was dreaming about a new, more powerful mechanical computer that would be the marvel of the age.

Ada Lovelace, a gifted young woman who also happened to be the daughter of poet Lord Byron, immediately grasped what Babbage was trying to accomplish. It's believed that Ada helped Babbage develop the way in which the Analytical Engine could be addressed and programmed. Their relationship, intense and familial, would last nearly two decades.

Like modern computers today, Babbage intended his machine to have two main parts:

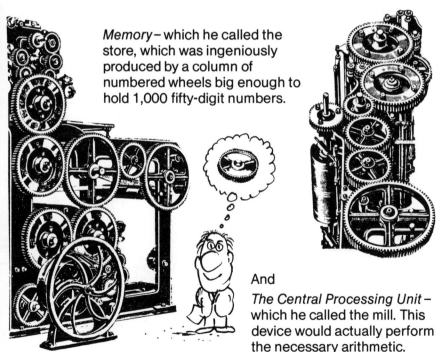

Memory– which he called the store, which was ingeniously produced by a column of numbered wheels big enough to hold 1,000 fifty-digit numbers.

And

The Central Processing Unit – which he called the mill. This device would actually perform the necessary arithmetic.

Punch Cards, another innovation, would be the way that the machine could be programmed to follow the steps it must perform. These steps, similar in function to a cooking recipe, are called *algorithms*.

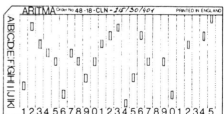

Amazingly, punch cards were still being used to program computers and input data up until the 1960s and 70s.

The cards were actually the invention of a Frenchman, Joseph Marie Jacquard (1752–1834), who used them to control a textile loom. In Jacquard's machine, the cards were rolled on a drum where a series of metal rods sought the holes punched in them. When a rod found a hole, it rose; otherwise it remained stable. The movement up and down created a pattern, in much the same way that a similar action in a player piano or music box creates a melody.

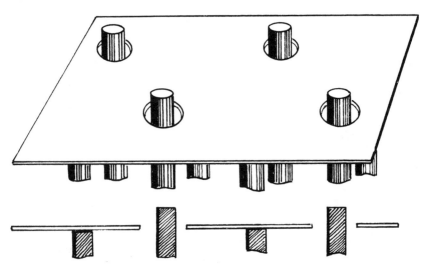

Babbage was so impressed by the card system that he acquired an intricate portrait of Jacquard woven by an astonishing 24,000 cards.

"The Analytical Engine weaves algebraic patterns just as the Jacquard loom weaves flowers and leaves."

– Ada Lovelace

Alas, the Engine never wove a thing.

Babbage never raised sufficient funds to build a working machine. And Ada, unhappily married, became a compulsive gambler, alcoholic, and cocaine addict. She died in 1852, at age 36.

The last giant step toward the modern computer was taken in the USA by an inventor who was as practical as Babbage had been visionary...

Herman Hollerith (1860–1929), who always finished what he started. Again it was necessity that fathered a great invention. The urge to count heads goes back to ancient Babylon, where 30,000 clay census tablets have been found dating to 3500 BC. But in the United States, a census every ten years was actually mandated by law – since the number of Congressmen each state possessed was based upon its population.

EVERYONE IS A NUMERIC UNIT FOR EXAMPLE I AM THE NUMBER ONE!

Taking the census became a major problem as the US population soared from 2.5 million in 1776 to more than 60 million in 1890. Yet the method hadn't changed much from Babylonian times: making tally marks on slips of paper.

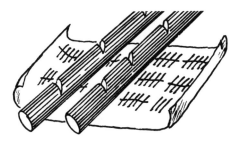

Complicating matters further, the US Census was more than a head count. Questions about race, sex, age, work, and home added to the paperwork. Like Babbage before him, Hollerith hit on the idea of using punch cards to record and store data.

"I was traveling in the West and I had a ticket with what was called a punch card photograph... the conductor... punched out a description of the individual, as light hair, dark eyes, large nose, etc."

– Hollerith

This was done to discourage the use of stolen tickets.

Hollerith decided to put the information about each citizen around the borders of the card. Later he invented a keyboard device for quick punching, and an ingenious electrical tabulator to read the results.

	Own home	Rented accom.	Living in a barrel	Home-less
Income group 1	O			
Income group 2		O		
Income group 3			O	
Income group 4				O

It was the first use of the new electric technology in computing. Each time the tabulator "read" a hole punched in a card – for age, sex, birthplace, and so on – an electrical connection registered on an appropriate dial. Some dubbed the invention a "statistical piano".

And it worked. In a single 24 hour period, the mostly female census tabulators recorded complete data for 6,711,590 people. This was the first large-scale use of women in the office workplace.

Hollerith's machine made it possible to analyze previously unimaginable masses of statistics. Its invention is also considered the beginning of modern data processing – so essential to today's computer revolution.

In 1911, two decades after the triumphant 1890 census, Hollerith merged with two other companies that manufactured business machines. The new firm was called the Computer-Tabulating-Recording Company. Thirteen years later, with Hollerith in retirement, the company changed its name to International Business Machines...

IBM. A name forever associated with the Computer Age just about to begin.

Chapter III
ELECTRIC DREAMS: THE RACE TO CREATE THE MODERN COMPUTER

*"If I have been able to see farther than others, it
was because I stood on the shoulders of giants."*
— Sir Isaac Newton

Up until the middle of the twentieth century, people could still think
of scientific progress as a kind of orderly human pyramid spanning
the ages. No longer. Modern computer science has developed so
rapidly, with so many different inventors making important
contributions often at the same time, that perhaps a better image to
keep in mind is that of a spirited pile-up on a football field.

This story begins in 1940, with Europe at war and the USA preparing for the inevitable. The National Defense Research Committee is hastily formed to produce advanced weapons of war. But instead of creating a giant centralized think tank, government funds are funneled into university research programs around the country.

The approach was typically American – and still is the case today. At the cost of redundancy, wasted effort, and isolation among the scientists involved, the gamble paid off in unparalleled creativity and invention.

The Committee's theoretical research eventually led to the creation of the atom bomb. But on the more practical level, it still had to deal with the nagging military problem of making accurate firing tables for America's big guns. After all, even the best new artillery has to be aimed correctly. That meant taking into account the type of cannon, the projectile, the fuse, gravity, and air densities. Plotting a single trajectory could take 750 separate calculations.

To do the job, the Army used the Mark I, an early computer built by IBM. The machine was a 100 ton collection of shafts, gears, and wires that sound like a room full of tin crickets when it works.

The Mark I kept count with a new invention called the relay or
flip-flop. It was just a small metal bar attached to a spring that was
triggered by a magnet when electricity passed through – something
like the clanger of a doorbell. Each relay represented a certain
number. It stayed open when no electricity passed through it. But it
quickly switched closed when it received an electric pulse, which
registered the presence of that number.

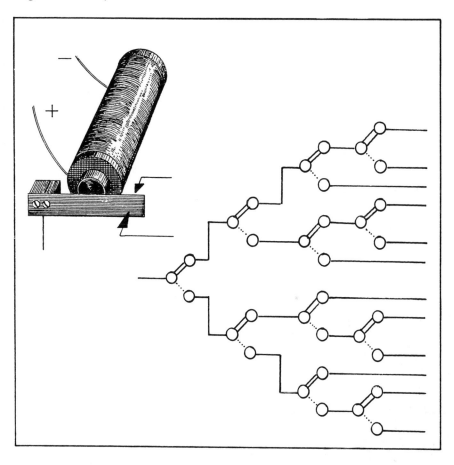

The relays were connected to each other. When two numbers were
supposed to be added together, current passed to the relays set
aside for those numbers. Those relays then closed, triggering a third
relay – which represented the sum of the two numbers. The way it
worked was that if the flip-flops for number 1 and 2 switched closed,
the flip-flop for number 3 closed automatically to keep score.

Ingenious, but also clumsy. The many mechanical parts in the big clunker kept slipping out of place. Sometimes it took 3 days to solve a problem. Something faster was definitely needed. A pair of scientists at the Moore School in Philadelphia, J. Presper Eckert and John Mauchly, took an entirely different approach:

Electronics. Why couldn't flip-flops be made out of the vacuum tubes used in radio. Tubes were fairly expensive, used a lot of power, and often failed because of inadequate cooling. But they could also switch on and off very, very rapidly – thousands of times a second. The plan was to connect the tubes in relays, arranged in groups of 9. In a sense, each group of 9 tubes functioned the same way as the ones, tens, or hundreds columns of the abacus. When the numbers to be added exceeded 9, the tubes in the ones group switched off and the first tube in the tens group switched on.

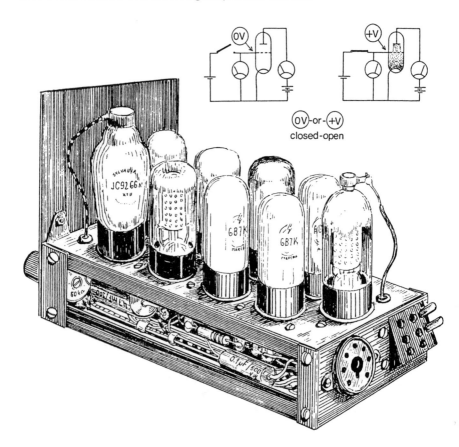

(0V)-or-(+V)
closed-open

By 1942, Eckert and Mauchly were able to land a government contract to build a totally electronic computer that could calculate trajectories in minutes. The machine was dubbed the Electronic Numerical Integrator and Computer – ENIAC for short.

Meanwhile over in England, a secret research center had been set up on a large estate in Bletchley Park, near London. Here too the demands of war were producing a breakthrough in the application of computer science...

CODE NAME: ULTRA. A Jewish refugee who had worked on a sophisticated German decoding machine before the war escaped to England with the plans recorded in his memory. A working model was built and studied at Bletchley Park.

Alan Turing, a gifted young mathematician, used this information in the creation of COLOSSUS, probably the world's first working electronic computer. The machine's sole purpose was to crack the German code. It worked perfectly. Using 1,800 vacuum tubes, COLOSSUS could deal with up to one trillion possible code combinations.

PROJECT ULTRA's computer was used to help Britain eavesdrop on German war plans. Its importance was so great and its existence so hush-hush... that it is said that Prime Minister Churchill could not warn the people of Coventry that they were about to be bombed, for fear of tipping his hand. Historians are still debating today whether or not Turing's computer actually won the war.

Back in the USA, ENIAC was complete. It was a metal behemoth containing 40 separate instrument panels, 17,000 vacuum tubes, and 6,000 switches. Its dimensions were nearly 100 feet long, by 10 feet high, by 3 feet deep. But it was fast. ENIAC could multiply two numbers in under 3 milliseconds – that's 3 one-thousandths of a second. It could complete a trajectory in 30 seconds. And it needed only 2 hours to complete a problem that would've taken 100 trained men a whole year to solve manually. In short, ENIAC was more than a thousand times faster than any previous computer.

IT'S BIG! IT'S FAST!

BUT IT DRIVES ME BANANAS!!!

It could also be programmed to do different jobs – unlike COLOSSUS, for example, which was *dedicated* to the task of decoding. Unfortunately, ENIAC had very little internal memory. Every number required a separate tube to hold it. That left fewer tubes to do the work.

J. Presper Eckert, now at MIT, suggested using a piece of quartz crystal that oscillated when electricity passed through it. When tubes containing the quartz were linked together in a loop, the circuit "remembered" that it had been charged.

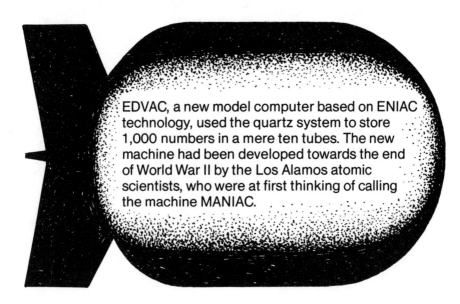

EDVAC, a new model computer based on ENIAC technology, used the quartz system to store 1,000 numbers in a mere ten tubes. The new machine had been developed towards the end of World War II by the Los Alamos atomic scientists, who were at first thinking of calling the machine MANIAC.

John von Neumann, an extraordinary Hungarian-born mathematician involved in nuclear research, brought a theoretical grasp of computer science and flamboyant showmanship to the new technology. In articles and speeches he convinced the government to support new computer development. His personal popularity was so great that the term Von Neumann Machine became synonymous in the press with computer.

After the war, Eckert and Mauchly teamed up again to build an even more sophisticated machine. Jokingly called the Indiscreet Numerical Fudger and Computer (INFAC), it was officially named the Universal Automatic Computer.

To several generations of Americans, it was familiarly known as UNIVAC.

It was intended to put computer power into the hands of government and such businesses as insurance and market research. The A. C. Nielsen Company, known today for their TV rating service, were one of UNIVAC's first customers. But costs rose during development, and Eckert and Mauchly were forced to sell out to a much larger firm. Eckert was able to keep working on UNIVAC for his new bosses. But Mauchly was assigned to sales.

ALL SANE AMERICANS HAVE THE RIGHT TO ASSOCIATE THEM-
-SELVES WITH FLYING SAUCERS!

Why? Just the facts, lady. The year was 1949, and the Cold War and McCarthyism had descended on America. Mauchly was denied security clearance to work on his own invention because 20 years before he had unknowingly attended a meeting of an organization deemed subversive.

In 1951, UNIVAC was finally ready. Input and output were no longer through clumsy punch cards. Magnetic tape, like that used in today's cassettes, was used to send commands and data into the machine. Compared to ENIAC, it was one-tenth the size, ten times as fast, and able to store 100 times the information. It was very simply the best computer then in existence.

In 1952, UNIVAC showed tens of millions of American TV viewers what it was capable of doing. In a daring public relations move, Remington Rand Company, the computer's new owner, offered to predict the outcome of the Presidential Election between Eisenhower and Stevenson. Like the rest of the newsmen at CBS Network Election Eve headquarters, Walter Cronkite was extremely sceptical:

> "We're not depending too much on this machine. It may just be a side show."

Engineers programmed UNIVAC to study past voting records over 25 years. News reports started coming in at 6:00 pm and were duly entered into the machine. By 9:00, UNIVAC predicted a landslide victory for Eisenhower – while the majority of human experts were still projecting a tight race.

CBS was afraid to announce the computer's conclusion. So the engineers reprogrammed the machine along more cautious lines. It didn't matter. UNIVAC still rated Ike's chances of victory at better than 100 to 1. When final results came in later that night, it turned out that the computer had a margin of accuracy of 99 percent. As commentator Edmund R. Murrow said of the experiment, "The trouble with machines is people."

THEY WOULD PREDICT THAT THE NEXT CHAIRMAN WILL BE MAO!

WHAT THE HELL HAPPENS IF THE RED CHINESE GET A COMPUTER!?

Computers suddenly became a big business. Companies that once made adding machines and cash registers now took the plunge into the new technology.

Other firms began to split up and spawn a flock of fledgling computer companies – that soon also took off. A prime example is UNIVAC which begat Control Data, which in turn begat Cray Computers. This pattern would repeat itself many times over the next 20 years.

Yet computers were still too large, too expensive, and too slow for many uses. And the vacuum tubes they depended on were still too hot, too prone to burn-out and other failure. A major technological breakthrough was necessary to create the next generation of computers:

The transistor. Unlike most other computer pioneers, the men responsible for this discovery were not clever inventors, engineers in love with the way machines work, or mathematicians who needed a better way to calculate. They were physicists engaged in "pure research" at AT&T's Bell Labs, and their names were Walter Brattain, John Bardeen, and the controversial superstar of the group, William Shockley.

LOUIS ARMSTRONG COULD NOT HAVE INVENTED THE TRANSISTOR, BUT HE COULD HAVE HIS SPERM FROZEN!

In later years, Shockley would get involved with wild theories about the genetic superiority of the white race and eugenic schemes to freeze the sperm of geniuses for future artificial insemination. But in the late 1940s and early 1950s, Shockley and company were much more interested in the properties of the then- mysterious materials called *semiconductors*.

Used today in all computer chips, semiconductors do exactly what their name implies. They don't conduct electricity easily like metals such as copper. Nor do they completely block the flow of electrons like nonconducting insulators such as glass. What they do is conduct electricity in a single direction.

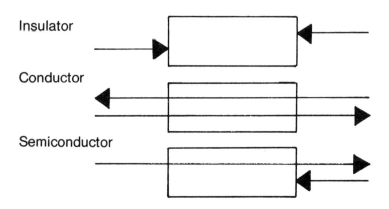

Insulator

Conductor

Semiconductor

This makes them useful as amplifiers in stereo equipment and pocket radios. But it also makes them the perfect replacement for vacuum tubes as electronic switches in modern computers.

Semiconductors today are made from substances such as gallium arsenide, germanium, and the most plentiful substance on earth, silicon, the main ingredient of sand.

By themselves, these semiconductor materials do not conduct electricity. Their crystaline atomic structure is too stable, with too few or no free electrons to pass electrical current. Yet when they are *doped* or intentionally contaminated by other chemicals, they can be made to perform in very special ways.

Doping takes two forms. In the first, an element is added that has free electrons, such as arsenic. In the second, a "hole" is created by adding an element like boron which has one less electron than silicon.

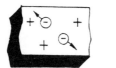

Put these two kinds of semiconductors together, and you create an electronic valve or *gate.*

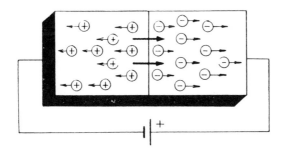

Electric current flows in, but it's kept from alternating back and forth by the barrier created between the two doped crystals.

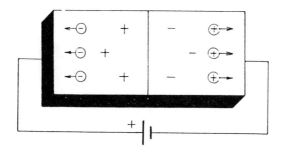

When a small electric signal is applied to the semiconductor, it actually amplifies that signal. And what you have is a *transistor*, a device that transfers resistance, technically speaking. The Bell Labs team's first primitive transistor could amplify an electric signal as much as 50 times. But soon transistors were also being linked together in computers to serve as super-fast electronic relays.

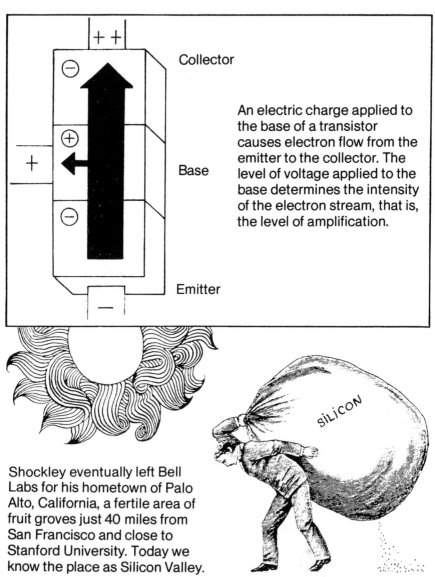

Collector

An electric charge applied to the base of a transistor causes electron flow from the emitter to the collector. The level of voltage applied to the base determines the intensity of the electron stream, that is, the level of amplification.

Base

Emitter

Shockley eventually left Bell Labs for his hometown of Palo Alto, California, a fertile area of fruit groves just 40 miles from San Francisco and close to Stanford University. Today we know the place as Silicon Valley.

Stanford had created a sprawling industrial park next door to the University in order to build a bridge between science and business. Two graduate engineering students, William Hewlett and David Packard, had laid the groundwork for this development in the late 1930s by forming an electronics company in their garage – the computer age's answer to the artist's garret.

WELL, THE WORKSHOP'S FINE, BUT THE BUICK'S GETTIN' RUSTY!

In 1957, a group of Shockley's employees bolted his company, got outside financing, and formed Fairchild Semiconductor, a billion dollar operation today. This kind of entrepreneurship became the model for most other Silicon Valley companies. It even gave our language the term "spin off", a new enterprise that has spun off from an existing one.

THIS SPIN OFF IS GOING TO BE A REAL MONEY SPINNER!

The new computers made with transistors were much smaller, faster, and even cheaper than the ones using tubes. But each transistor still had to be separately wired together with many others in a circuit. And each electronic component might need several hand-soldered connections. All it took was a few faulty connections to make even the most powerful computer – with several hundred thousand electronic elements – absolutely useless.

Super computers being planned for the US Space Program were expected to require as many as 10 million separate electronic parts. How could such a device be tucked away into the tip of a rocket? How could all the transistors involved be tested beforehand? Who could design such a complicated system of circuits?

Computer science had come face to face with a limitation as serious as the Sound Barrier had proved to aerodynamics:

The tyranny of numbers. As many of us know today, the solution to that problem was the silicon computer chip. But to one of the co-inventors of the chip, engineer Jack Kilby at Texas Instruments, the solution was known as the Monolithic Idea.

Since individual transistors were being made of doped silicon, Kilby wondered if a single piece of silicon could be used to create *integrated circuits*. These would include other essential components such as resistors and capacitors, also made from doped silicon.

On September 12, 1958, Kilby's first primitive integrated circuit or IC was successfully tested. It was a half inch wafer of semiconductor, deposited on glass, and crudely wired together. Needless to say, it worked.

At almost the same time in California, one of the founders of Fairchild Semiconductors, was also trying to overthrow the tyranny of numbers. On January 23, 1959, Robert Noyce wrote in his notebook:

Noyce came up with the idea of depositing thin strips of metal directly on the chip, thus eliminating the need for wiring. For this contribution, Noyce is recognized as the co-inventor of the integrated circuit, along with Jack Kilby.

Modern computer chips are marvels of design and miniaturization. A silicon flake less than 1/4 inch thick can hold millions of microscopic electronic components -- over ten times more than the 30-ton ENIAC. The most advanced chips can even perform millions of separate calculations per second.

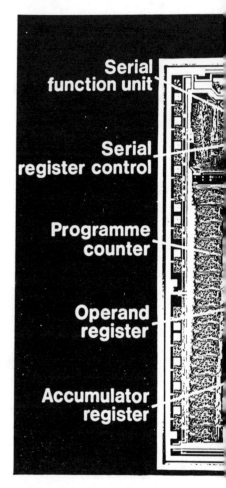

Serial function unit

Serial register control

Programme counter

Operand register

Accumulator register

Each area performs an important function. The *addressing unit* keeps track of where various bits of information are stored or can be placed. In the computer, coded information in the form of numbers is moved from location to location. Each place has an "address" which is itself a number – like the street number on a house.

The ALU – arithmetic-logic unit – is the main work area of the chip. As the name implies, it is here that the actual counting and logical processes (such as comparing two numbers) take place.

ROM – read-only memory – contains specific instructions and working data that are built into the chip when it is made. The user cannot "write" new data into ROM – hence the name. Simple chips that control single processes, in an automatic coffee machine, for example, only require this kind of memory circuits.

RAM – random access memory – allows the user to store data and program in the computer. It's the working memory of the machine, since it can be used to "write" as well as simply "read".

An integrated circuit like the one below is small enough to be carried by an ant, yet it can hold as many names as a big city telephone directory. Under a microscope, it resembles nothing more than an aerial view of an urban metropolis, complete with streets, plazas, and gigantic building complexes.

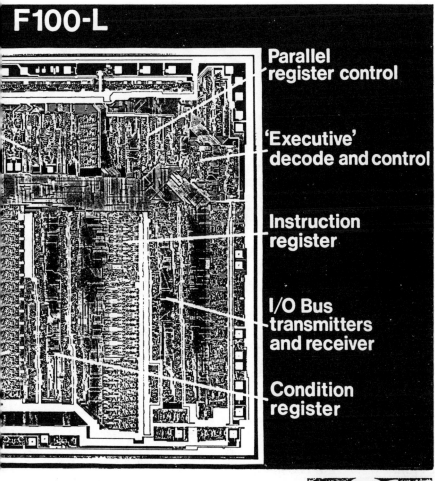

F100-L

Parallel register control

'Executive' decode and control

Instruction register

I/O Bus transmitters and receiver

Condition register

Buses – metalic electric pathways – connect all the areas together like a mass transit system or network of highways.

All this intricate circuitry is manufactured by a complicated, expensive industrial process called *photolithography*. But first the pattern of the chip must be designed. Engineers draw up detailed plans on large pieces of drafting paper many times the size of the finished chip.

In recent years, computers have been enlisted in this process. Technicians input diagrams of transistor patterns, rules about how to link them, and a description of how they're supposed to work.

THE QUESTION NOW IS: HOW TO MINIATURIZE THE OPERATOR!

The computer then designs the chip's maze of circuits, displaying them on screen, and testing them by running simulated operations. Errors in the circuitry are hunted down electronically and removed.

I AM NOT A COMPUTER BUG! I AM AN ORDINARY HOUSE MITE READY FOR THE CAMERA!

In another part of the factory, long crystals of purified silicon are sliced into thin wafers. Each wafer may produce hundreds of separate chips. The chips are coated with a protective oxide, and are now ready to have the circuit pattern inscribed on them.

68

The silicon is first treated with a light sensitive plastic. Then the outline of the circuits is superimposed using ultraviolet light, which causes the plastic to harden. Acids dissolve the unprotected areas. More silicon is layered in, treated with the impurities that give it the necessary semiconductivity, and then the process is repeated.

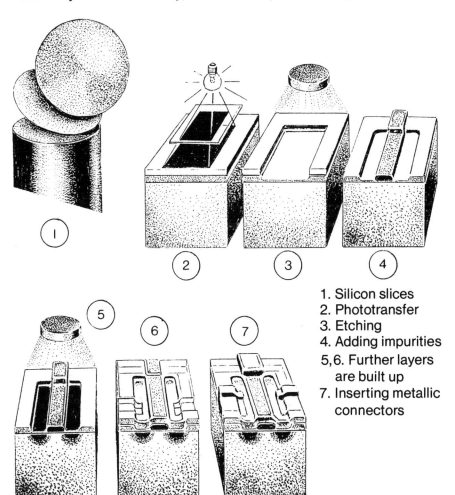

1. Silicon slices
2. Phototransfer
3. Etching
4. Adding impurities
5,6. Further layers are built up
7. Inserting metallic connectors

Successive layers of semiconductors are created. Cut away areas produce "windows" which are filled with conductive metal condensed right on the chip. Finally, the completed chip is cut from the wafer. It is connected to wires, and placed in a protective case with electric prongs that can be snapped into place.

The obvious superiority of the new IC chip technology convinced even the usually cautious IBM. The company that had begun with Hollerith was slow to get rid of their punch cards and vacuum tubes. But after spending billions of dollars, in 1965 IBM introduced its revolutionary model 360 computer that utilized the new chip technology. They quickly gained a commanding share of US and international markets. Powerful machines like these were dubbed *mainframes* because of their large central processor and array of peripheral accessories.

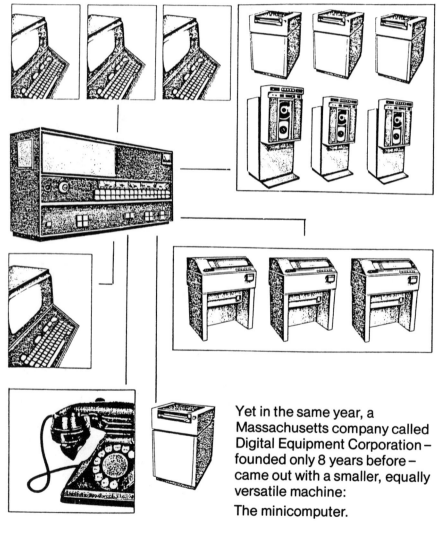

Yet in the same year, a Massachusetts company called Digital Equipment Corporation – founded only 8 years before – came out with a smaller, equally versatile machine:

The minicomputer.

Suddenly government, science and business had an entirely new menu of choices.

Spin-off followed spin-off in the computer business. In 1970, INTEL, a California company that sprang from Fairchild, discovered how to put the brains of the computer - the Central Processing Unit or CPU - right on one chip.

The microprocessor was born. And dozens of new companies - some operating out of garages and basements in Silicon Valley - began to exploit the new technology.

Since the 1970s, there has been an explosion of new devices controlled by tiny computer chips. Some of the "smart products" have entered our lives in the form of automatic washing machines, cash registers, cameras, stereos, CD players, music synthesizers, and video games.

Apple Computers, founded on a shoestring by two computer hackers only in their twenties, rose from a garage to a billion dollar corporation on the strength of the small, powerful, easy-to-use microcomputers. The era of the Personal Computer or PC had begun, and soon dozens of other computer-related companies sprang up all over the world. Their goal was to put a smart machine in every business and nearly every home.

In the 1990s, an estimated one out of three American families have a computer in their homes. Yet as computer companies battle for a share of this market, some worried that demand for new and better machines has already peaked.

Were computers just another fad? Like hula hoops, pet rocks, or roller disco?

Companies around the world are investing billions of dollars on research for the next generation of computers. Imagine machines that can understand spoken language and speak back, machines that are faster and easier to use than any other devices in history.

Machines with almost human smarts.

ALMOST HUMAN?! HE PERHAPS THINKS IT IS A COMPLIMENT!

Why not? If anything is true about the history of computers it's that anything is possible.

Chapter IV
BITS, BYTES & BINARY: HOW COMPUTERS WORK

For many people a computer is just an empty *black box* that performs electronic wonders as if by magic. That's OK. After all, you don't need to understand the thermodynamics of the internal combustion engine to learn how to drive a car.

Yet it's really not hard to understand the basics if you take them in slowly. This knowledge will help you comprehend what computers can and cannot do. Besides, since computers are central to modern technology, it's certainly worth the try.

Big *mainframe* systems used in government, scientific research, and business work on similar principles as a perky little *microcomputer* in someone's home. So let's begin there.

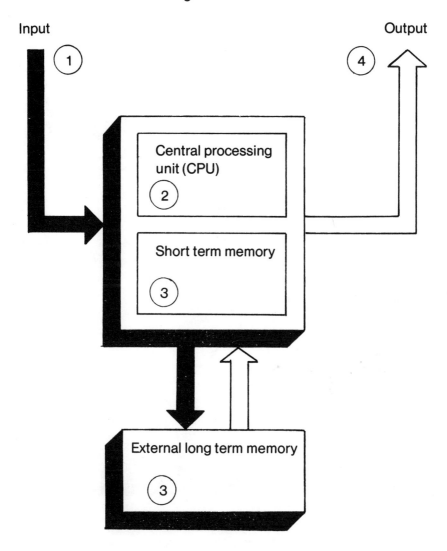

Input

Output

Central processing unit (CPU)

Short term memory

External long term memory

Information moves through any computer in four basic stages. It is (1) input; (2) organized by the processor; (3) stored; and (4) output in a new form.

INPUT

Input is what you put into the computer. It usually takes the form of numbers or words typed in by keyboard. But input can also be a wiggle on a joystick in a computer game, a temperature reading coming from a sensor in a washing machine, a pattern of pulses from a TV camera, or a burst of electronic data from another computer sent over phone lines.

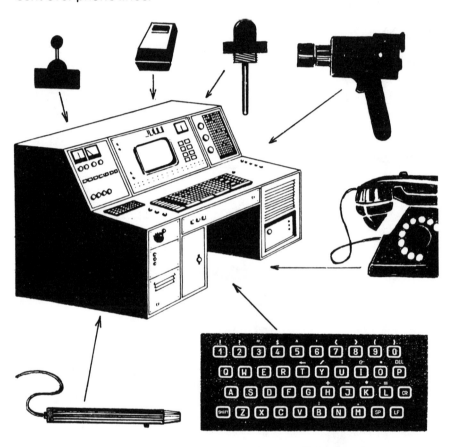

Another kind of input is the *program* – the steps the computer will take to do various jobs. With the right program you can find the square roots of numbers, draw color pictures, move a robot around the room, or plot the best route from one end of town to the other. In most home PC's, the program is usually *loaded* into the computer's working memory on or after start up. The program is stored in the form of small plastic discs or cassette tapes.

THE PROCESSOR

The Central Processing Unit (CPU) organizes the input. It regulates where and how information will flow through the computer, according to the steps laid down in the program. In this sense, the processor is like a traffic cop who directs certain cars to a factory parking lot, tells others to wait, and waves priority vehicles like fire engines down express routes.

MEMORY STORAGE

The computer contains its own short-term working memory. This is designated as RAM - random access memory. It's also used to store interim data while a complicated computer operation is still going on. A computer's power is often measured in terms of how many megabytes (Meg) of RAM it possesses. Each meg represents the ability to store 1,024,000 numbers or letters in active memory. Some PCs today come with 16 megabytes of RAM or even more.

The computer can get to its active, working memory quickly and easily. RAM, however, is *volatile*. This means that it disappears when the machine is turned off. That's why long-term memory is stored outside the computer. Older machines used flexible "floppy" disks and even cassette tape to store data. Today's computers use sturdier magnetic disks for storage, as well as *hard drives* capable of saving and retrieving hundreds or even thousands of megabytes.

OUTPUT

Output is the processed information that the computer puts out to you. Most commonly this takes the form of words and numbers displayed on a monitor screen or written on paper via a high speed printer. But output can also be the computer's commands to another machine – home appliances, a satellite in orbit, or a robot arm in a factory.

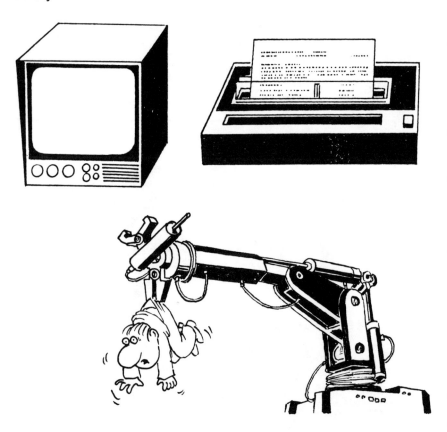

The heart and brain of the computer is the Central Processing Unit (CPU). Some years ago it consisted of piano-sized boxes full of vacuum tubes or transistors. Today's CPU comes in the form of a powerful silicon chip called the microprocessor, usually less than 5mm or two-tenths of a square inch. This tiny chip can contain millions of electronic circuits.

The microprocessor has several important functions. There's an *input/output* area because it must communicate with other parts of the system. There's a *control* area that regulates what the computer does and when.

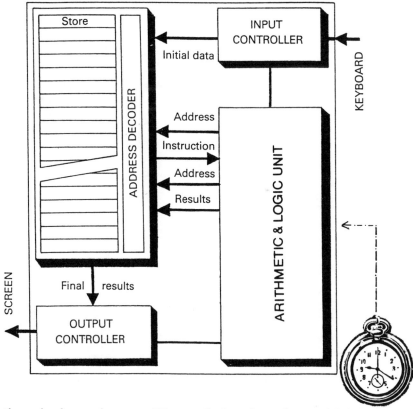

A tiny clock produces millions of electric pulses which keep the entire system working together.

The working part of the chip is the arithmetic-logic unit or ALU. Deceptively simple, it can perform only four elementary tasks:
1. adding
2. subtracting
3. transfering data in and out of storage, and
4. comparing

Yet the ALU can perform these functions at speeds over a million times a second. So what it lacks in cleverness, it easily makes up in speed. Technically, the ALU consists of special circuits called adders, registers, and counters. Here's how they work:

An *adder* receives data from two or more sources, combines them, and sends the result to a register. A *register* receives data, holds it, and transfers it as directed by the processor. And a *counter* keeps track of the number of times an operation is performed.

Why keep track? Because a computer multiplies and divides the way we did as children – by adding and subtracting. For example:

$$8+8+8+8+8+8=48$$

Which is another way of saying 8 x 6 = 48. As children we learned to count on our fingers. How does a computer count? Or do anything?

Each of the thousands of electronic circuits in a computer can switch on and off incredibly fast. When a pulse of electricity flows through a circuit, we say it is *on*. When no electricity flows through it is *off*. On circuits have a value of 1; off circuits have a value of 0. Make sense so far?

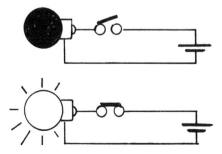

The computer does all its calculating and processing with only these two numbers. 1 and 0 are the basis for the *binary* number system used in practically all computers.

Each number is called a *bit*. That's short for *bi*nary digi*t*. The computer only needs the two numbers of the binary system because everything it *reads* is translated into combinations of 1 and 0. When the computer receives a command read as 0, it turns off a certain circuit. A command read as 1 tells the computer to turn a certain circuit on.

Computers usually deal with strings of 8, 16, or 32 bits at a time. These strings are called *bytes*. The computer translates letters, numbers, and symbols into bytes which it can recognize and process. Larger bytes send more information through the system faster.

Every time you press a key on the computer keyboard, you send a sequence of coded voltage "on-off" pulses into the machine.

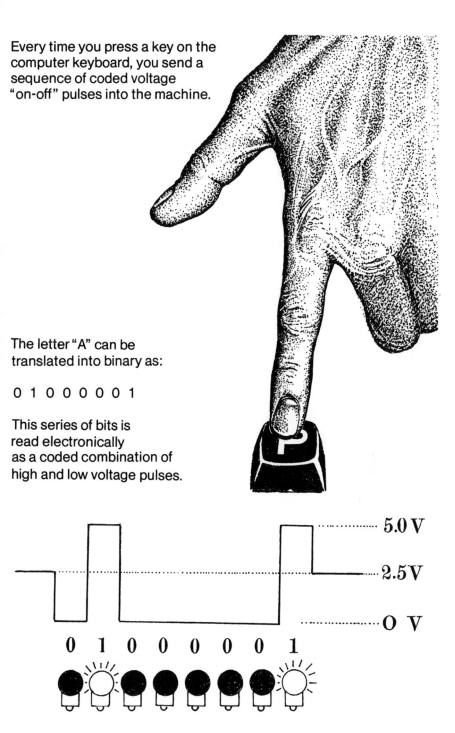

The letter "A" can be translated into binary as:

0 1 0 0 0 0 0 1

This series of bits is read electronically as a coded combination of high and low voltage pulses.

5.0 V

2.5 V

0 V

0 1 0 0 0 0 0 1

A similar idea is behind Morse Code, in which letters and numbers are represented by a combination of long and short strokes on a telegraph key.

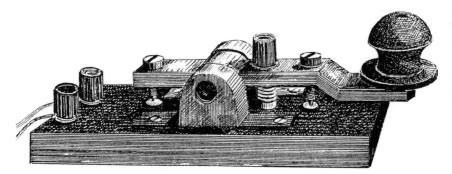

All the letters in the alphabet, numbers 1–10, and important symbols such as =, −, +, and $ are listed as 7 bit codes in the American National Standard Code for Information Interchange – ASCII, pronounced As-key. This standard is used in computers throughout the Americas, Europe, Japan, and the rest of the world.

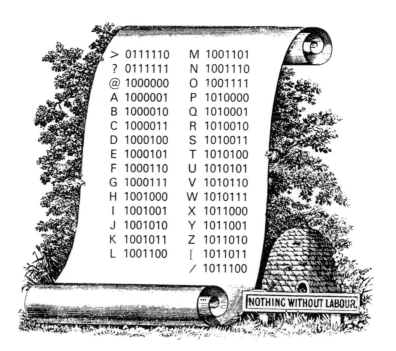

> 0111110   M 1001101
? 0111111   N 1001110
@ 1000000   O 1001111
A 1000001   P 1010000
B 1000010   Q 1010001
C 1000011   R 1010010
D 1000100   S 1010011
E 1000101   T 1010100
F 1000110   U 1010101
G 1000111   V 1010110
H 1001000   W 1010111
I 1001001   X 1011000
J 1001010   Y 1011001
K 1001011   Z 1011010
L 1001100   [1011011
           / 1011100

NOTHING WITHOUT LABOUR

For people it's easier to use the decimal numbers one through ten. Counting in decimal is based upon organizing numbers in terms of 10s, 100s, 1000s, and so on. These are called the *powers* of ten.

Ten to the 1st power (10^1) means 10 x 1 $= 10$
Ten to the 2nd power (10^2) means 10 x 10 $= 100$
Ten to the 3rd power (10^3) means 10 x 10 x 10 $= 1000$

Binary uses a similar system of powers, based on the number 2.

Two to the 1st power (2^1) means 2 x 1 $= 2$
Two to the 2nd power (2^2) means 2 x 2 $= 4$
Two to the 3rd power (2^3) means 2 x 2 x 2 $= 8$
Two to the 4th power (2^4) means 2 x 2 x 2 x 2 $= 16$

Here's how the number 13 looks using the binary system:

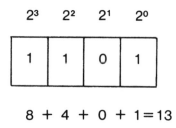

$$2^3 \quad 2^2 \quad 2^1 \quad 2^0$$

1	1	0	1

$$8 + 4 + 0 + 1 = 13$$

Using only the eight bits in a byte, we can count up to 255.

$$2^7 \quad 2^6 \quad 2^5 \quad 2^4 \quad 2^3 \quad 2^2 \quad 2^1 \quad 2^0$$

1	1	1	1	1	1	1	1

$$126 + 64 + 32 + 16 + 8 + 4 + 2 + 1 = 255$$

And by using only 16 bits, we can count all the way up to 65,535.

The Binary System was the invention of George Boole, a self-taught English mathematician, who showed how two numbers could be used to express complex kinds of arithmetic and logical statements. Today's computers utilize Boolean logic to calculate and make decisions.

The processor uses the coded zeros and ones – the presence or absence of electrical current – to operate circuits filled with tiny transistor switches. These switches are arranged in special ways to create several kinds of controls called logic *gates*. Two typical controls are the AND and OR gates. This is a simplified model of how they work in the computer:

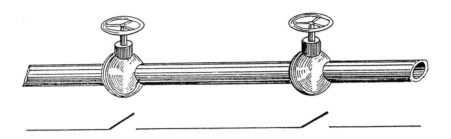

The AND gate passes electricity through its circuit only if both of its incoming wires are switched on.

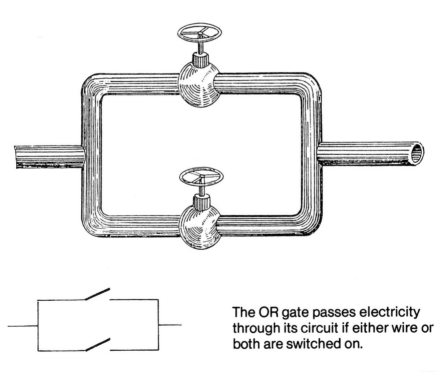

The OR gate passes electricity through its circuit if either wire or both are switched on.

You can find a good example of how an AND gate works at the bank's computerized teller machines. A person will receive money if two conditions are met:

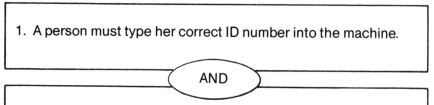

1. A person must type her correct ID number into the machine.

AND

2. A person must have sufficient funds in her account to cover a withdrawal.

Entering the correct ID number will send electric current through one wire. Having sufficient funds will send current through a second wire. The AND gate now opens completely. RESULT:

An OR gate works if either wire sends current to the gate. A good example might be an alarm system installed in a home.

Once the system is activated, the alarm will ring if a window *or* a door is opened from outside.

In reality, a microprocessor depends on various combinations of these and other logic circuits. But you might find yourself relying on your computer's AND gates if you were conducting a search for people who live in Cambridge and also speak Czech. And the computer's OR gates might come in handy if you are monitoring an industrial process in which a foul up on any of the steps could mean disaster.

Computers are surprisingly easy to use if you have the patience to learn the rules. The first rule is that you run the computer, and not the other way around. Basically, the machine doesn't have the faintest idea what you want it to do until you tell it. And you usually tell it by typing in instructions or by making choices from a *Menu* of things the computer is programmed to do.

When you begin an art program, for instance, the machine will put a menu on the screen that might ask if you want:

1. to create new pictures
2. view the pictures you made the day before
3. read the instructions that tell you how to create new pictures
4. choose a different program

THE BEST INSTRUCTION TO CREATE NEW PICTURES IS A DECENT ADVANCE PAYMENT!

Say you make your choice and type in Number 1 on the keyboard. The computer may then put up a second menu on screen to find out if you want to use your light pen or some other means of drawing a picture. Other menus will come up on screen whenever you have to make a decision.

Computers are programmed to help people solve many different kinds of problems – ranging from the best way to budget your pay to the best way to coordinate traffic lights in a big city.

The computer can't make these decisions alone. People have to input the information the machine needs to evaluate alternatives. And people also have to analyze and structure the problem so that it can be solved, just the way they would if they were making decisions without the computer.

Here's a simple example. Say you want to avoid getting soaked by the rain. What do you do? You might follow these steps:

1. Look out the window

2. Decide – is it cloudy or rainy?

3. If it is, take an umbrella

4. Go out

A convenient way to visually represent problem solving is the *Flow Chart*, in which decision steps are laid out in a logical order. Notice that the Chart *branches* whenever a decision must be made between two or more things.

Here's a simplified chart dealing with the Problem: Should I carry an umbrella?

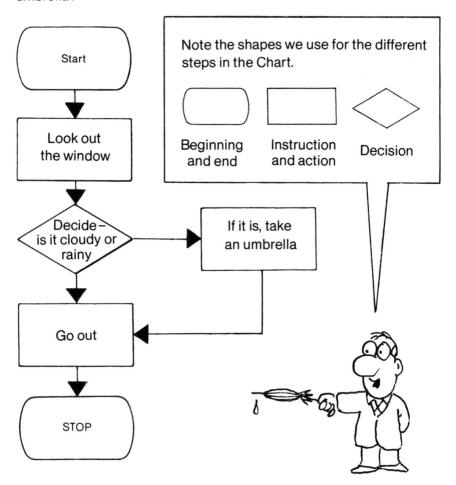

Most of us solve simple problems like this in our heads. But for more complicated decisions, flow charts become important reasoning tools. To efficiently use a computer or to program it, this kind of organization can be critical.

Now let's take on a computer-sized problem. And a realistic one at that. Travel agencies around the world are often asked to decide the "best" route from one place to another. Nowadays they use computers to help them.

Say we're talking about a trip from a city called Northgate to a resort called Southport. We've already stored every possible route in our computer's memory, along with schedules and other information. Now we've got to determine what "best" means, and decide which route and mode of travel – bus, train or plane – best fits this description.

Is best cheapest?
Fastest?
Prettiest?
Let's get specific. Our customer specifies that the trip shouldn't cost more than $50, take more than 3 hours, or go through any polluted industrial areas. All this in mind, your flow chart might look like this:

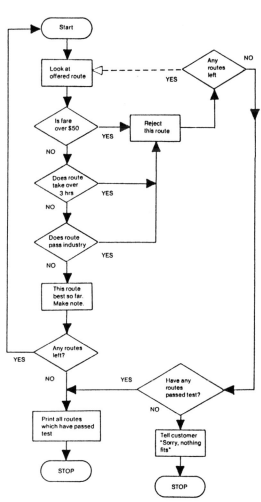

As you can see, this Chart works by a process of elimination. If we were thinking of going by plane, the fact that the fare costs more than $50 would eliminate it from consideration. Or if we were wondering about the bus, the fact that its route takes it through the factories of Quarryville would also put it out of the running.

In our analysis, only the train meets all three criteria.

PROGRAMMING

Flow Charts come in handy when you're programming the computer to solve problems of any kind. A computer program is a series of instructions which are loaded into the computer as a whole. For this reason, it's not necessary to give an instruction, wait for the machine to carry it out, and then give another and another.

AND WHEN YOU ARE FINISHED, GO AND HAVE A NICE CUP OF TEA!

Computers can deal with sophisticated problems because most programs are designed to deal with possible alternatives or branches. This means that anything you might want the computer to do has to be broken down into simple steps. Also each command must be written in *language* the machine can understand.

Programming language uses a special set of code words to tell the machine what you want it to do. BASIC, designed at Dartmouth College in 1964, is the language programmers first used with small computers. It's still important today. Essential codes include:

 REM – for remark. This command lets us write comments for our own use into the program. The computer, however ignores any line beginning with REM.

 PRINT – tells the computer to display the words that follow on the screen. Words and numbers that follow this command must be enclosed in quotation marks.

 $ – nope, not money. The sign tells the computer not to change anything that precedes it.

 INPUT – tells the computer to ask the user for more information. Puts a "?" on screen where an answer is required.

 END – obvious. Tells computer it has reached the end of the program.

Using these code words, a simple program can be typed in like this:

```
10. REM    This program gets a name and uses
           it to greet us.
20. PRINT "Welcome to programming."
30. PRINT "What is your name?"
40. INPUT name$
50. PRINT "Hello,"; name$
60. END
```

After each command you must press the RETURN key. (Also called the ENTER, CR, or NEWLINE key on certain machines). This tells the computer to accept the command as input.

Now that you've finished typing, your program will appear on screen like this:

Welcome to programming.
What is your name?
? WOZ
Hello, Woz

WOZ ?! MEIN NAME IST HUBERT!

Did you notice that in the program each line was numbered in increments of 10? The numbers let the computer store the command in a specific memory address, and retrieve it when needed. The gaps between the numbers – 10 to 20, for instance – allow you to write in any additional commands that occur to you.

Right. Now, in more ambitious programs we need a few more code words:

IF... THEN – it says what it means. If whatever follows the IF command is true, THEN we are given special instructions. Otherwise, we just move ahead to the next line in the program.

GOTO – tells the computer to jump ahead to a specified instruction in the program.

These code words would appear in program looking something like this:

```
100. PRINT "Please give password."
110. INPUT  password$
120. IF password$ = "BASIC" THEN GOTO 150
130. PRINT "Please run program again."
140. STOP
150. PRINT "Naturally, come right in."
160. STOP
```

In plain English, the program tells the computer to ask the user for the correct password. If she types in BASIC, then she is told to come right in. Otherwise, she is asked to try again. So far so good?

Not only are programs agonizingly complex and tedious to write, it is ridiculously easy to make a mistake in numbering a command, spelling it, or phrasing it. These errors are called *bugs*. Debugging a program can sometimes take as much time as it took to write it in the first place.

Like other computer languages, there are several different *dialects* of BASIC. One kind may require you to type GOTO as GO TO. Unless you've written your commands using the correct *syntax* for your dialect, you won't accomplish very much.

Fortunately, thousands of programs written by other people are now commercially available for practically every purpose imaginable, from predicting sunspots to spotting spelling errors on a word processor.

Besides BASIC, here are a few other important computer languages:

FORTRAN – developed in 1954, the name stands for "FORmula TRANslation", which is precisely what it was developed to do. FORTRAN translates math formulas and problems into language the machine can deal with.

COBOL – or COmmon-Business-Oriented-Language. It was invented in 1961 to process data used in business.

PASCAL – named after mathematician Blaise Pascal. This language is more difficult to use than BASIC, but it helps reduce programming bugs by compelling programmers to think and write more clearly. Each computer operation must be broken up into small blocks with definite beginnings and ends.

LOGO – often used in schools to teach young people how to make computers perform simple, but interesting tasks.

PERIPHERALS

Here are many of the add-on features that make it easier for the user to communicate with the computer, and vice versa. These peripherals are commonly used in connection with the smaller Personal Computers found in homes and businesses. Specialized peripherals used in science, big business, and government will be featured in the next chaper.

But first a word about the *Small Computer System Interface* (SCSI). The "scuzzy" ports or sockets at the back of the computer allow you to connect the computer to other peripherals. This interface slows down the speed of computing, yet it greatly increases the computer's versatility.

INPUT

ICONS

Icons help create a user-friendly computer environment. It's no longer necessary to learn whole lists of commands and to type them every time you want the computer to do something. You point your mouse at an icon and click. The computer does the rest.

Both Apple Computer's Macintosh and Microsoft Windows use a variety of icons to represent different functions: a file holder, a calculator, a clipboard, a graph, margins, and even a trashcan -- to mention a few. Art programs display icons showing pencil, paint brush, air brush, dotted line, eraser, as well as different patterns and colors.

Rather than typing out what you want to do, icons let you choose simply by pointing. This is done by moving the *cursor* – a square blip on screen – with the aid of the arrow keys on the keyboard. Or . . . you can use a peripheral like:

The Joystick or The Mouse

When these devices are hooked up to the computer, they allow the user to "steer" the cursor right to an icon or some other part of the screen where a decision is called for. (You can use the cursor to choose from a list of options on a menu.) The joystick – a computer game standard – works similar to ones used in airplanes. The mouse has a small ball under it which guides the cursor when you roll it across a table.

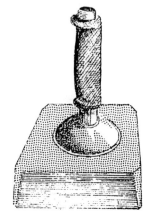

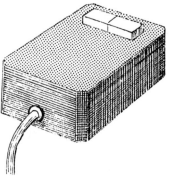

Light Pen

Sophisticated machinery and programs let the user point right at a choice with this device. It is also widely used to produce computer pictures, graphics, and other art. When used with appropriate software, the computer screen is transformed into a digital grid. Moving the light pen across the outside of the screen tells the computer, for example, to draw an analogous line on the inside surface of the screen.

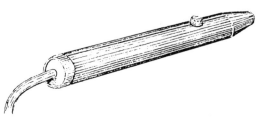

OUTPUT

PRINTERS

Printers let the user transfer information from the screen onto paper -- also known as *firmware*. Letters, envelopes, reports, graphs, and spreadsheets are only a few of the uses. The fastest printers use laser technology; excellent results are also available from less expensive "bubble jet" printers. Older dot-matrix printers produce letters, numbers, and designs by combining patterns of dots on the page.

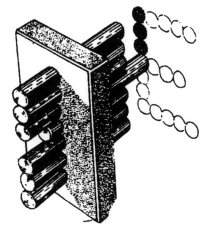

PHONE HOOKUP

The modem works to extend the reach of your computer anywhere phone lines or satellites can take you. It is used extensively today for both input and output. The modem connects your machine with the vast international computer network called the INTERNET, as well as electronic bulletin boards and databases around the world. You can both send and receive anything that can be produced electronically: writing, reports, games, art, and scanned pictures. In the past, computers depended on exterior modems, connected to the telephone receiver. Most modern computers, however, come equipped with faster built-in modems.

Despite the difficulties of trying to deal with a machine on its own terms and in its own language, today's computers have a power and flexibility that would've made it the envy of pioneers like Charles Babbage, who spent a lifetime in the pursuit of a device that could truly be a universal problem solver.

Chapter V
MAJOR MUSCLE:
COMPUTERS IN ACTION

"If the shuttle would weave and the pick touch the lyre without a hand to guide them, chief workmen would not need servants, nor masters slaves."

– Aristotle

Until the 1970s, most people had never seen a computer chip close up. The big mainframe machines of those days were treasured, pampered, and locked away in air-conditioned citadels. There they were maintained by an elite caste of data processing High Priests in starched white shirts -- that era's answer to Pharoah's corps of computating scribes.

In contrast, modern computers are found everywhere. One reason is price. Today's smaller, cheaper machines outperform the clunky mainframes of the past. In recent years, steady technological advances have cut the cost of computing an estimated 50% every year.

Consider this. A system that might've cost $2 million in 1960, $200,000 in 1970, and $20,000 in 1980 -- today might cost less than a couple of thousand dollars. Plus, you don't need an engineering degree to use it. If motor car technology had progressed at the same rate, a Rolls Royce would be going for around $30 nowadays.

IT WOULD BE A BARGAIN!

$ 30 —

The other main reason is flexibility. Computers are found nearly everywhere today because they easily link up with other machines. True, computers are very useful for helping people store and retrieve information relating to other people. Electronic filing systems are quickly replacing paper in most large institutions such as government, utilities, hospitals, and schools. Yet the most exciting new applications of computer technology involve direct machine:machine *interface*.

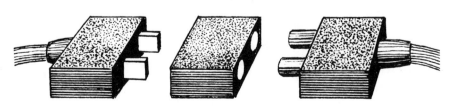

COUNTING

Computerized cash registers speed the check-out line along at the supermarket. The device scans the lined *bar codes* on the products whisked past its electronic eye. The register automatically adds up the price of all items, tacks on tax, and even makes change.

9 780723 570462

Academic testing companies and many colleges use computers to cut the time involved grading student exams. A photoelectric sensor compares multiple choice responses with correct answers stored in memory. The computer then adds up the result and spits out a grade.

Similar systems are used in banks for keeping accounts.

Without computers, it would've been difficult or even impossible to have performed all the calculations necessary to plot the course of space probes like the Voyager project, programmed to intersect the orbits of Jupiter and the outer planets on its billion-mile journey to the end of the solar system and beyond.

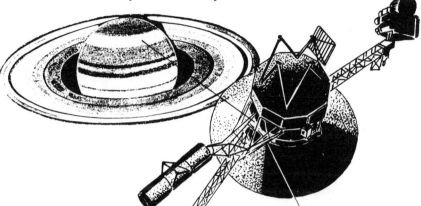

Other types of calculation try to predict possible events before they happen. The US Weather Service uses powerful super computers like the Cray II to calculate the force and direction of hurricanes and storms. These forcasts affect thousands of lives and billions of dollars of property.

Engineers also use computers to calculate the strength of various designs and building materials. These are then compared with possible environmental stresses that might occur, such as strong winds and quakes.

CREATING MODELS

Approximately 60% of that part of the brain called the cerebrum is involved with interpreting visual information.

This in mind, it should come as no surprise that images can be powerful stimulants to thought.

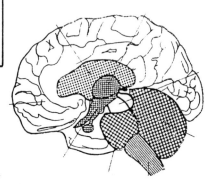

It is said that Einstein began thinking about problems of relativity after imagining himself travelling on a beam of light. Many physicists and mathematicians today also claim to think in terms of visual models – not numbers. Here are some of the ways *computer graphics* can help to understand and solve complicated problems.

Since 1984, the US Olympic Team has used computers to train athletes. First, top competitors are filmed going through their paces: pole vaulting, diving, or hurling a discuss. The computer then scans each frame of film, breaking up complex motions into simple parts. Stick figure models of the athlete in action are produced on screen. These figures help other athletes to discover the most efficient ways to train.

Computers can show us more about things than commonly meets the eye. Anything that can be detected, analyzed, and measured can be depicted graphically. Astronomers are now able to train radio telescopes and other sophisticated sensors at the stars to detect a variety of energy forms other than visible light: radiowaves, microwaves, infrared, and ultraviolet. The computer then interprets this data to create dramatically enhanced models of what's really going on in the universe.

Computer technology is also used to study human biology like never before. CAT (computerized axial tomography) and PET (positron-emission tomography) scans use X-rays and low-level radiation to explore the inner workings of the body. From relatively small amounts of data, the computer is then able to construct color-coded models of what's really going on under the skin. This kind of information can extend doctors' understanding of biology, and help them to more effectively treat patients.

Computer graphics are also put to work simulating complicated processes, such as flying an experimental plane or running a modern steel mill. In this way, possible problems can often be detected in advance and corrected. Human personnel also gain experience operating complex systems without the risk and expense of practicing in real life situations.

- MUST BE A GALLSTONE! HE CAN'T BE PREGNANT!

CAD or Computer-Aided Design creates electronic prototypes of new products and machines, from running shoes to racing cars. Designers use a light pen or *drawing pad* connected to the computer to sketch in the basic shape and components. The system then takes over, filling in the design and even rotating the image in three dimensions. Alterations can be made almost instantly and tested on screen without having to go back and create physical models.

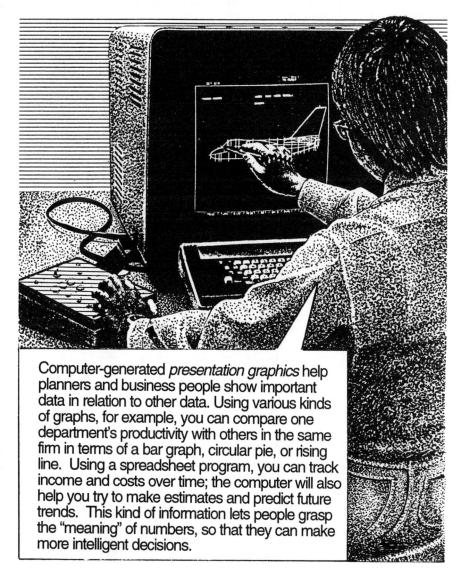

Computer-generated *presentation graphics* help planners and business people show important data in relation to other data. Using various kinds of graphs, for example, you can compare one department's productivity with others in the same firm in terms of a bar graph, circular pie, or rising line. Using a spreadsheet program, you can track income and costs over time; the computer will also help you try to make estimates and predict future trends. This kind of information lets people grasp the "meaning" of numbers, so that they can make more intelligent decisions.

Word processing with computers takes a lot of the drudgery out of writing and editing.

The system involves a keyboard, a computer with memory, a video monitor, and a printer. Typed words appear on screen, where they can be quickly edited or altered electronically. Punctuation, spacing, type face, and paragraph order can all be changed before the printer puts a word on paper. Some programs even correct spelling. The finished page is usually stored externally on diskette or in the computer's hard drive.

Electronic mail is mainly used for communicating from one company or department to another. Letters and memos are sent via phone wires or satellite from one computer to another, where the message appears on screen. This removes a good deal of delay and cost.

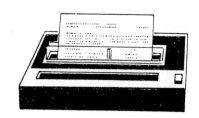

Videotext is a relatively new service offered by pay TV networks all over the world. It uses computer graphics instead of video pictures. Weather, sports, stock market reports, travel information, and educational features are often available on different channels. In some areas, it is possible to shop and bank by computer. And in Columbus, Ohio, a system called QUBE lets users vote at home on various issues.

Digital technology based on computers is revolutionizing entertainment. Special effects generators used in films like STAR WARS produce incredibly realistic other-worldly images. Digital televisions now under development will allow viewers to run scenes in slow motion, freeze frames, zoom in, or divide the screen into multiple images – so that more than one channel can be watched at once. This technology will also greatly improve reception by computer-enhancing images and electronically removing distortions like "ghosts" and static.

Digital recording uses computers to convert sound waves into patterns of on–off pulses. This system removes distortions like tape hiss and loss of fidelity.

The digital signal is then electronically "etched" onto a compact disk, which can be read by laser. The original quality of the sound will never fade or be marred by scratches. Digital technology will soon also be used to improve telephone communication and boost the effectiveness of hearing aid devices.

Computers are now being used to coordinate interaction between people and machines.

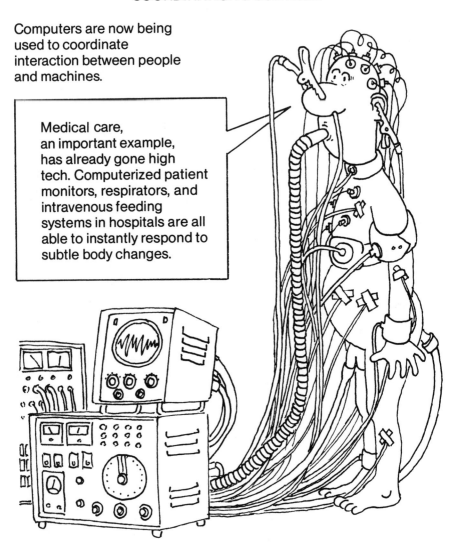

Medical care, an important example, has already gone high tech. Computerized patient monitors, respirators, and intravenous feeding systems in hospitals are all able to instantly respond to subtle body changes.

In the area of machine:machine coordination, modern telecommunications would be impossible without sophisticated satellite guidance and tracking. Today, most phone companies use computers alone to link caller and receiver. And within advanced factories, refineries, and processing plants, computers monitor and control crucial industrial factors like temperature, flow of raw materials, and general product quality.

Finally, small microprocessor chips are used to control the electrical and fuel injection systems of cars and other vehicles, in order to maximize fuel efficiency. *Smart products* like automatic microwave ovens, home thermostats, videotape recorders, telephone answering machines, and heart pacemakers would all be unthinkable without miniaturized computer control.

CONSTRUCTION

Tens of thousands of working robots are now in use around the world. They have little in common with the two-legged metal humanoids we've grown to fear and love in the movies. Most resemble giant mechanical arms attached to rolling gas pumps. They cannot see, walk or talk. And with the exception of a few experimental models, their only function is to labor in heavy industry - spray painting, welding, screwing bolts, blending chemicals, and pouring molten metals. These are all tasks that are difficult, dangerous, or basically boring for humans.

The working part of the robot is usually a "hand" made of three jointed digits that can swivel, press, and operate tools. The most advanced Japanese factories are now totally robotised. Dozens of robot arms working in unison manufacture an unceasing flow of autos, cassettes, and even other robots.

These machines are also being developed for use outside the factory. Mechanical miners may one day dig metals underground. Robot undersea vessels are currently being used to explore the ocean floor at pressures that would crush a fragile human diver. And a flexible robot arm built in Canada has been put to work on the Space Shuttle to repair and launch communications satellites.

A robot containing its own computer brain may soon be sent to other planets in the form of a self-propelled exploratory vehicle. The Mars Rover, as it is called, will use video sensors to see. It will also be able to move around or over obstacles in its path, collect mineral specimens, analyze them, and even plot its own course across the Martian surface.

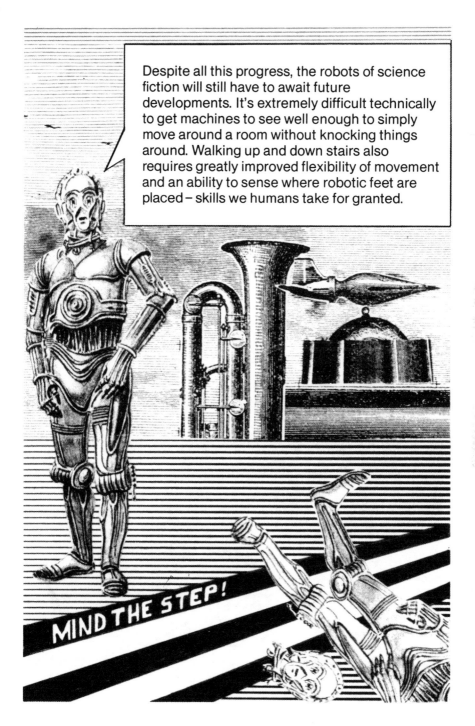

Despite all this progress, the robots of science fiction will still have to await future developments. It's extremely difficult technically to get machines to see well enough to simply move around a room without knocking things around. Walking up and down stairs also requires greatly improved flexibility of movement and an ability to sense where robotic feet are placed – skills we humans take for granted.

MIND THE STEP!

There is no question that the computer's ability to count, calculate, create models, coordinate and control, and construct products has already made this technology an essential part of today's world.

Yet many people have not ceased to worry about the price we may have to pay for the accomplishments of the Computer Revolution. Fantastic visions of rampaging robots and dictatorial electronic brains are not all that these critics have in mind. There are a host of other possible dangers, less colorful but more possible, much closer at hand.

Chapter VI
UPSIDE/DOWNSIDE:
SURVIVING THE COMPUTER AGE

"The bigger the front, the bigger the back."
> – Zen saying

The computer is a tool, an extension of the human mind, senses, and limbs. And like all tools, it's only as good as the people who use it.

No one would doubt the value of fire. Looking back over history, we know that it has been used to clear land for farming, cook food, smelt metals, bake pottery, stay warm, and even send smoke signals.

But people have also used fire to devastate an enemy's cities and brand him as a slave.

IT ALSO HELPS WITH THE CONFESSION!

Another problem is that even when a powerful tool like the computer is conscientiously applied to good purposes – not everyone will benefit equally. In other words, one person's upside can often be another person's downside. Consider these examples.

WORK

In the early 1800s, during the Industrial revolution, an army of working people gathered under the banner of Edward Ludd to smash the high technology of that time – the mechanized textile looms, workshops, and factories being constructed all over England.

Known to history as the Luddites, these industrial rebels futilely tried to turn the clock back on the machines that threatened their jobs, their position as skilled workers, and their sense of self-esteem.

"No General But Ludd Means The Poor Any Good"

In the years that followed, great fortunes were made from industrialization. Eventually the benefits of the Machine Age even spread to many workig people in Europe and the US. But the human costs were terrible. Millions labored under hellish factory conditions for bare survival. Unemployment was chronic and actually used to keep wages low. The skilled worker who once took pride in craft was now reduced to slavishly servicing the machine.

WHAT'S WRONG? NEITHER I NOR MY RELATIVES, FRIENDS OR COLLEAGUES HAVE MADE A FORTUNE!

Nowadays, many people are again worried about what will happen to their jobs as a result of the Computer Revolution. Are these fears realistic?

First the upside. Nearly half of all the productivity gains in the US since World War II are linked to technological improvements, including the computer. Until the 1980s, greater productivity tended to create more jobs. Most of this growth centered on the service and information industries, where wages can range from a low of a few dollars per hour for a dishwasher to several hundred for a financial consultant.

What about manufacturing? Get ready for the downside. A study by Stanford University predicted that "robots could replace up to 3 million jobs" by 2005. Here's why: A $50,000 robot doing the work of one person costs only $6 an hour to run, compared with the $20+ needed to cover a blue collar worker's salary and benefits. Steel collar robots also never organize troublesome labor unions, demand profit sharing and safe working conditions, or take coffee breaks or vacations. Unfortunately for employers, robots don't buy manufactured goods either.

Then what about all the jobs that will be created in new high tech industries? Sorry, but it's estimated that jobs created by this sector will not even equal half of the 2 million manufacturing positions already lost in recent years. Worse, computerization may soon affect many white collar workers too. As companies automate, computers are expected to take over many current supervisory and accounting functions. And intelligent *expert* computer systems programmed to make basic decisions may one day replace tens of thousands of highly-paid middle managers.

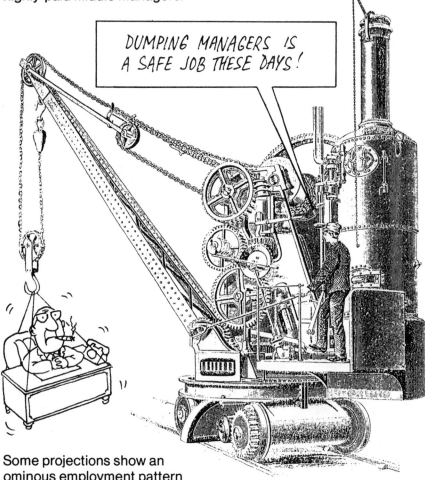

DUMPING MANAGERS IS A SAFE JOB THESE DAYS!

Some projections show an ominous employment pattern developing over the next 20 years.
As technology eliminates the need for skilled workers outside the computer field, a two tiered occupational structure may be created.

A few handsomely-paid professionals, technicians, and business managers will stay on top. Most of the rest of us will be on the bottom.

WORK IS A PRIVILEGE OF OUR CLASS. COMMUNISM WOULD DESTROY IT!

The US Labor Department predicts that the real growth area for jobs in the future will be unglamorous service positions like janitors, hospital orderlies, and security guards. Computer mechanics – the fastest growing high tech category – will need only one-eighth as many people as categories such as fast food workers and kitchen helpers.

YES, EVERYBODY WOULD HAVE TO WORK!

DON'T PANIC. These are only projections, after all. New technologies are not always put into place as quickly as technically possible. High initial costs, training, and employee resistance cause many companies to go slow.

But the writing is on the electronic wall for many of us. Some of the questions we might want to ask about the future include these:

★ How can we make sure that the benefits of high tech productivity are shared among all members of society?

★ Who will buy the houses, cars, and other high ticket items so important to the economy if many formerly well-paid workers are forced into low-paid jobs?

★ If society is divided into technological haves and have-nots, can democracy still function?

124

THE ENVIRONMENT

Unlike old-fashioned smoke stack industries, computer manufacturing is safe and clean, right? Unfortunately, that myth simply won't wash. High tech industries will never produce the *volume* of pollution created by large steel mills, car plants, or refineries.

The downside is that industrial pollution from chip manufacture is probably even more toxic.

In the 1980s, a report by the California Division of Occupational Safety and Health found three times the normal rate of illness among workers in Silicon Valley. Roughly half the sicknesses resulted from exposure to toxic chemicals used to produce semiconductors:

arsenic – from silicon doping
hydrofluoric acid – from photolithography
polyurethane plastic and highly toxic PCBs –
   from chip encapsulation
nickel oxide and cyanide salts – from chip
   electroplating
cadmium and lead oxide – from chip bonding and
   soldering

These substances have been directly linked to cancer, bone destruction, skin and eye irritation, kidney damage, lung scars, reproductive hazards, anemia, and brain damage.

But the stuff's safe if it's handled and stored properly, right? In a perfect world, perhaps. Toxic leaks at Fairchild Semiconductor's waste storage facilities released 58,000 gallons of a poisonous chemical, TCA, into the Santa Clara, California water system. Levels of this dangerous substance were 30 times the safety level.

In Silicon Valley alone, more than 100 leaks and spills have already been reported. The effect? An epidemic of miscarriages and birth defects two to three times the norm. The situation is potentially even more dangerous in the developing nations of Asia and Latin America, where many computer components are now being produced and assembled. Safety precautions in these foreign plants are often far below the US standards. Worse, workers and the public in these countries may have little voice or power to improve conditions.

Identical environmental hazards have also been discovered near semiconductor plants in Massachusetts and Virginia.

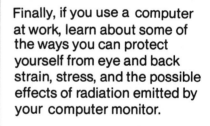

DON'T PANIC. Organize. Elect public officials who have a good record on environmental issues. If you live near a high tech manufacturing area, join with your neighbors to insist on safe waste disposal techniques and frequent inspections by government agencies. If you actually work in the industry, explore the role that organized labor unions can play in educating employees about job safety and protecting them from hazards.

Finally, if you use a computer at work, learn about some of the ways you can protect yourself from eye and back strain, stress, and the possible effects of radiation emitted by your computer monitor.

WAR

It might be argued that the high tech superiority of US and NATO forces reduced the number of troops needed to match Soviet forces in Europe during the Cold War. This, in turn, allowed America to build a leaner all-volunteer Army. And it may even have limited the tendency toward militarism found in nations with large standing armies.

Possibly.
Anyway, that's the upside.

Yet the downside of computerized warfare is otherwise very troubling in terms of costs, uses, and future risks. An estimated 50¢ out of every dollar the Pentagon spends on weapon systems goes for electronic components. This is one reason why today's aircraft, ships, tanks and other vehicles often cost ten times more than similar equipment just a few decades ago.

In the computer field alone, hundreds of millions of dollars are being spent on research into artificial intelligence. One goal is the creation of new "smart bombs" and other weapons that can be fired and forgotten -- and yet hit their targets. Other developments include the creation of the Army's proposed autonomous land vehicle, a robot "free fire zone" that drives itself and chooses its own targets.

Replacing flesh and blood soldiers with machines would certainly help to reduce American casualties in wartime. Yet it might also give generals the illusion that risk-free war is a real possibility.

The Armed Forces are funding the development of high-speed electronic decision-making systems. These were once a key part of former President Reagan's beloved Star Wars anti-missile space defense. Now they are being explored as ways of establishing command and control on the battlefields of the future, where things happen too fast for any human to make intelligent judgements.

Unfortunately, computers also make mistakes in judgment. In 1979 and 1980, computers of the North American Air Defense (NORAD) signalled false nuclear attacks on the US. The causes? In one case, a faulty circuit. In the other, a test tape simulating an attack was accidentally fed into the computer. Human intervention was fortunately close at hand to prevent the fatal counter-attack.

In the early days of nuclear weaponry, it might take hours for a manned bomber to reach its target. This allowed plenty of time to realize a mistake and call off a strike. Today, computer-guided missiles can reach their targets in as little as six minutes. This shrinking time frame makes a "launch on warning" strategy more attractive. The big question for the future is can we resist the temptation to let preprogrammed computer responses take the place of human judgment, where the safety of the world is at stake?

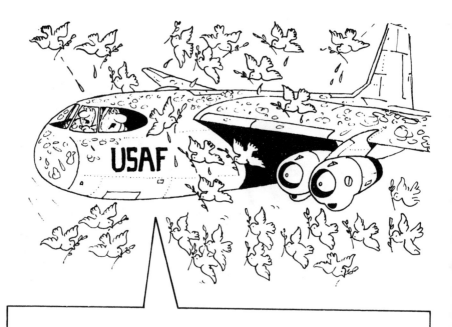

DON'T PANIC. Things are already complicated enough.

CRIME

Each day more than $1 trillion is electronically transfered over the world's financial networks. Computers make this amazing exchange possible. But they also make computerized crime, vandalism, and even terrorism an everyday reality.

Focusing on crime, the average bank holdup nets $15,000; the average embezzlement $25,000; but the typical computer heist scores an average of $500,000.

Yet even the enterprizing bank employee who *salami slices* a dime or two from the customer's transactions – and transfers it into his own dummy account – can clear tens of thousands a year.

The biggest scam of all amounted to $2.1 billion, and involved high ranking employees of a major insurance company who created fictitious policy records.

Other frauds have centered around phoney bank loans, pilfered railroad cars, imaginary savings deposits, misappropriated US Army supplies, bogus inventory, falsified advertising accounts, and invisible mutual funds.

Note that most of these rip-offs were inside jobs featuring company executives.

Who pays the cost? Less than an estimated 12% of all computer crimes are ever reported, and fewer than 1 in 10 criminals is convicted. Many of the financial institutions involved would rather swallow the costs – and take them out of the consumer's or the investor's pockets – than go public and risk a loss of confidence.

When credit card fraud is added in, computer crimes may total as much as $5 billion a year. The biggest risk of all is that a major fraud could lead to a company failure or investor panic, leading to a major market crash.

CBS CASHCARD

123456 789 012 345

Cambridge
Building
Society

A CARDHOLDER

BARCLAYCARD   VISA

4929 123 456

BARCLAYBANK

Politics, not profit, is the cause of other crimes. During the 1960s and 70s, student protestors sometimes attacked computers as agents of oppression. At the University of Wisconsin, one man died when a campus computer facility was bombed.

In Italy, commando units of the Red Brigades destroyed 10 computer centers during 1976 and 77. Their manifesto urged followers to "attack unravel, and dismember these networks of control". More recently, several similar raids were carried out by CLODO, a French terrorist group whose name means The Committee For Liquidating or Dismantling Computers. Members of this group claim to be disenchanted data processing workers who understand the current and future dangers of high tech systems.

In the USA, more than a hundred acts of sabotage have also taken place – but most are committed by lone individuals paying off personal scores.

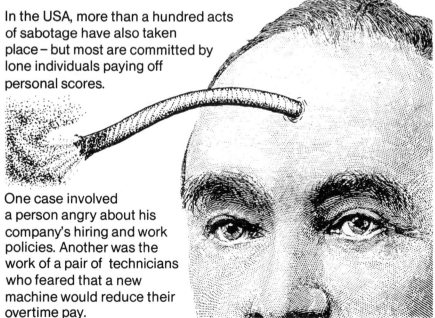

One case involved a person angry about his company's hiring and work policies. Another was the work of a pair of technicians who feared that a new machine would reduce their overtime pay.

At one European pharmaceutical company, the head computer designer tried to become indispensible by sabotaging his system from within. He secretly set *logic bombs* into his programs that would make important files disappear. In their place, the message "hello" popped up on screen. Naturally, only the logic bomber knew how to defuse his trap.

Logic bombs could also be potent weapons in the hands of international terrorists and blackmailers. The ten or so computers of the Federal Reserve banking system are one attractive target. Data need not be destroyed or physically removed. It need only be encrypted or coded, and held for ransom. A similar electronic attack against the air traffic control network could bring that form of transportation to a halt. Or simply by scrambling electronic codes for industrial orders, a terrorist working for one company could easy derail a competitor.

134

Computer pranks, not all of them illegal, have also raised the question of security. The popular movie WARGAMES showed how a young *hacker* could electronically break into the Pentagon's main computer and put US forces on red alert. Shortly after the release of the film, a group of Midwestern pranksters broke into more than 60 government and business databanks over the telephone. The group traded secret passwords and computer-access codes over the electronic *bulletin boards* that exist in most communities. All tnat was needed was a home computer, a modem, a phone, and some patience.

IF I ONLY KNEW WHAT WOULD BE BETTER FUN-STOCK MARKET CRASH OR WW III!?

Why do the hackers do it? One prankster felt it was a test or a challenge comparable to climbing a mountain. Another attacked the idea of making information a product for sale: "We don't believe in property rights."

"I disagreed with the system," explained a prankster at MIT. "It was fascist.
The people at the top were taking all the computer power. When I fixed it, I released some of the system's resources to all users."

Naturally, the people who own the databanks don't agree, and are trying to get laws passed to severely punish young techno-anarchists.

DON'T PANIC. New security systems are being developed to prevent serious acts of terrorism via computer. But as long as information databases are easily accessible to legitimate users – and that's one of their selling points – rebellious hackers will probably keep right on finding ways to share information with each other and the rest of us.

PRIVACY

Computer technology is now being used to catch fugitive criminals, reclaim stolen property, identify felons so they can't buy handguns, find fathers who've skipped out on child support payments, track down tax cheats so everyone pays a fair share, and even spy upon enemy agents who operate freely in our society. Yet the same systems that can be made to work for the good of all, pose a terrible threat to our privacy and freedom.

According to a widely discussed Gallup poll, nearly half of all Americans "believe that they now have little or no privacy because our government can learn anything it wants about them."

Paranoia?

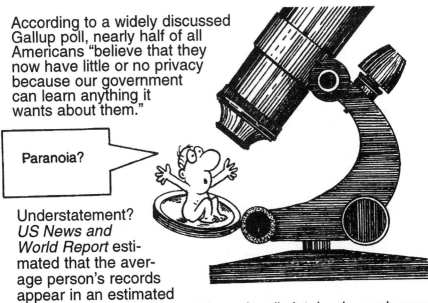

Understatement? *US News and World Report* estimated that the average person's records appear in an estimated 39 government (federal, state, or local) databanks -- plus an additional 40 private sector files. On a typical day, your name probably passes from one computer to another at least five times.

Officially, much of this personal information is restricted and private. Your credit rating, for example, is supposed to be confidential. So is your medical file, bank transactions, tax record, insurance history, and other data. But what happens when private companies share information about you with government agencies that in turn share it with other agencies and private companies? An electronic web is created, impossible to escape.

Consider this. The US Department of Health, Education and Welfare is negotiating contracts that will allow federal agencies to obtain 24 hours-a-day computer access to the credit ratings of citizens. This deal will also let the government swap loan information with private credit bureaus.

The Selective Service is buying and borrowing driver's license information from individual states, in order to locate young men who fail to register for the draft.

The Internal Revenue Service is trying to buy information from anyone about the names, addresses, and purchase history of citizens, in order to catch those who try to cheat on their taxes.

And the CIA, not to be left out, is continuing to be serviced by TRW, a huge multinational credit bureau with files on tens of millions.

But why should a good, law-abiding person fear that his or her personal life might be under scrutiny?

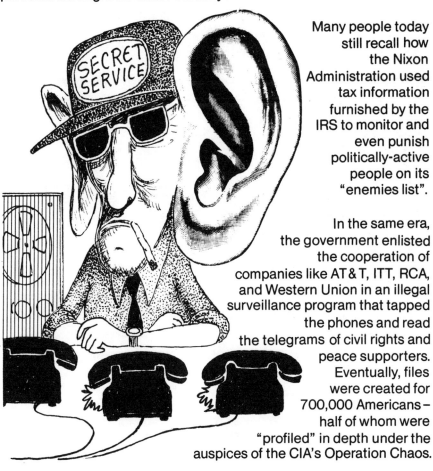

Many people today still recall how the Nixon Administration used tax information furnished by the IRS to monitor and even punish politically-active people on its "enemies list".

In the same era, the government enlisted the cooperation of companies like AT&T, ITT, RCA, and Western Union in an illegal surveillance program that tapped the phones and read the telegrams of civil rights and peace supporters. Eventually, files were created for 700,000 Americans – half of whom were "profiled" in depth under the auspices of the CIA's Operation Chaos.

So where's the harm in a little electronic spying? As one who wound up in the government file – along with people like Martin Luther King, Paul Newman, and Ralph Nader – Judge Abner Mikva replies:

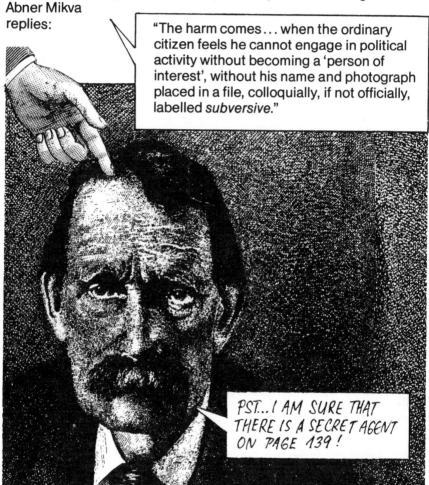

"The harm comes... when the ordinary citizen feels he cannot engage in political activity without becoming a 'person of interest', without his name and photograph placed in a file, colloquially, if not officially, labelled *subversive*."

PST... I AM SURE THAT THERE IS A SECRET AGENT ON PAGE 139!

But do people who are not politically active have anything to fear? Bringing things up to date, there is the National Crime Information Computer (NCIC). Its purpose is to track wanted criminals and stolen property across state lines. If your name turns up on NCIC, a police officer who stops you for a routine traffic check has the right to search, arrest or take other un-named measures.

A decade ago, the FBI asked for authorization to add to the NCIC database the names of people who are accused of nothing, but who are suspected of organized crime connections, terrorism, drug possession, as well as those who are "known associates" of drug traffickers.

If your name shows up on NCIC, you can be stopped, searched, surveilled upon, arrested, or worse. No warrant or court order would be necessary.

And because simply putting a name into the computer doesn't legally deprive anyone of liberty or property, constitutional due process law need not apply.

In a perfect world, the information in a databank would always be accurate and up to date. In the real world, however, things turn out differently.

One Californian was arrested and thrown into a military prison because a computer mistakenly reported him as a deserter. A Louisiana woman was locked up for theft and forgery because a computer check confused her with another person with the same name.

And a female Chicagoan was refused government job after job because her 20-year-old computer file quoted a 3rd grade teacher who claimed the woman's mother was crazy.

Private computer record services are no more reliable. One Los Angeles company provides tenant data to landlords. If you ever had a rent check bounce or you were served with an eviction notice – that a court later overturned – you may be refused a lease.

Each year roughly 350,000 people register formal complaints about the accuracy of huge TRW's credit reports. Nearly 100,000 succeed in changing the information listed about them in the company's computer. Yet, in most places, there is no law stating that a company is obligated to check the accuracy of the information it releases about you.

Making matters worse, because of the myth that computers are impervious to errors, many people blindly believe anything an electronic read-out says about anyone else.

BUT DON'T PANIC. Imagine what computers would do to life in societies where there is no tradition of law or freedom.

WELL, I WOULD HAVE HAD A VERY ACCURATE TAPE ON THE FIRST COMRADE!

As long as you are still free, make good use of your right to work for legal safeguards against arbitrary electronic surveillance by the government or private companies. The Freedom of Information Act and Privacy Act of 1974 entitles you to view the federal records kept on you. And the Fair Credit Reporting Act of 1971 gives you the right to see files kept by credit bureaus and other private companies – to ensure that they are accurate.

But in the Computer Age, who really cares? According to pollster Louis Harris, most of us, that's who. Especially, he adds, "when you touch that raw nerve end called privacy."

WE CARE!!!

Chapter VII
ARTIFICIAL INTELLIGENCE AND THE SEARCH FOR H.I.M.

Computers don't think. At least not the way people think. At least not yet. And they may never be able to do more than simulate elementary human thought processes. But this possibility has not deterred the thousands of researchers in the Artificial Intelligence (AI) field from searching for the key to the Hyper-Intelligent Machine or H.I.M.

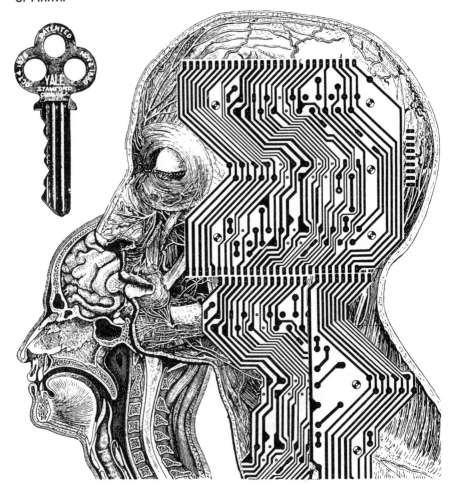

What is AI? The term was coined by mathematician and computer pioneer John McCarthy at a crucial information science conference held at Dartmouth College back in 1956. One of the highlights of that meeting was the unveiling of an early "intelligent" computer system called LOGIC THEORIST. This was much more than just a powerful *number cruncher* that could perform advanced calculation. LOGIC THEORIST worked with sophisticated mathematical symbols. The system was so smart and *cuspy* that it was able to produce formal proofs for several high level theorems that had intrigued such philosophers as Alfred North Whitehead and Bertrand Russell.

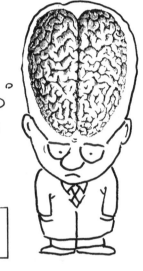

Ironically, no journal would publish these proofs because they were the product of a mere machine. Since that time, however, most people in and out of the AI field have tended to exaggerate machine intelligence. Based upon the early successes of systems like LOGIC THEORIST, predictions were made that computers would be outthinking people by the 1980s.

Clearly they aren't.

What happened? Before this question can be answered, let's imagine what a truly intelligent machine would be like. This will help illustrate how far computers still have to go.

HAL from the movie 2001 is most people's idea of a brainy machine.

HAL was remarkably intelligent. It – or he – could interface with humans in a *natural language*, English. It could see with the help of elaborate sensors, and interpret visual data in three dimensions. Not only could HAL do all the usual computer tricks – play chess, make calculations, communicate electronically with earth, guide a space vehicle, and run a complicated life support system – it could also read human emotions and simulate a few of its own. HAL, in other words, was good company on a long journey.

Aside from an unfortunate tendency towards mental breakdown, megalomania, and murder.

YOU ARE GIVING ME A HEADACHE!
I AM THE MOST NORMAL MAN IN THE
WORLD, EVEN WITHOUT YOUR PILLS, DOC!
WHAT'S WRONG WITH MURDER!?

Back in the 1950s, British mathematician Alan Turing proposed a test to evaluate computer intelligence. Turing claimed that a machine's success at carrying on a human-like conversation would be one good means of measuring smarts. Is it really? Read this conversation and decide for yourself.

THERAPIST: What's your problem?
PATIENT: I'm tired.
THERAPIST: Tell me more about such feelings.
PATIENT: I'm not alert.
THERAPIST: Did you come to me because you're not alert?
PATIENT: Yes.
THERAPIST: Are you sure?
PATIENT: Maybe I have other problems too.
THERAPIST: You don't seem quite certain.
PATIENT: Sorry.
THERAPIST: Don't apologize.

For the record, the therapist is being played by a computer program called ELIZA. It was developed at MIT in 1965 by Joseph Weizenbaum to show the possibilities and limitations of conversing with a machine via a keyboard. Weizenbaum intentionally used a pseudo-psychological framework so that a human would think a dumb question or wishywashy reaction was intentional.

One of the ways ELIZA accomplishes her illusion of intelligence is to transform the patient's statements using "I" and "my" into therapist questions using "you" and "your". When stuck for an answer, she simply poses stock questions such as, "Tell me more about…"

Unfortunately, ELIZA only appears to understand what is being said. Her program automatically scans for letters spelling "hi" and "who" – treating them as a greeting or question, even when they're really only part of a larger word.

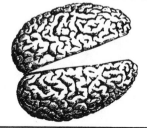

PATIENT:	I have a *who*le lot of problems.
ELIZA:	Why do you ask?
PATIENT:	I don't want to *hi*de anything.
ELIZA:	How do you do?

More about ELIZA's therapeutical career later. For now, it's enough to ask: What is intelligence? Few AI researchers or cognitive scientists can agree on an answer.

Is intelligence the ability to deal logically with problems? After all, unless the mind understands logical, mathematical concepts such as less and more, for example, it couldn't begin to compare even the simplest numbers.

Is intelligence having plenty of information about things? After all, you can't really know anything without the facts. And what does a statement like "The sky is blue" mean without knowing what the sky is and what colors are?

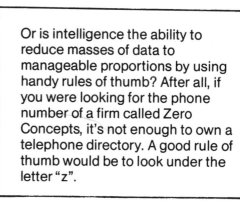

Or is intelligence the ability to reduce masses of data to manageable proportions by using handy rules of thumb? After all, if you were looking for the phone number of a firm called Zero Concepts, it's not enough to own a telephone directory. A good rule of thumb would be to look under the letter "z".

Real intelligence is a combination of all these factors, plus a number of mysterious human skills and strategies that are hard enough to identify and describe – let alone duplicate in a machine.

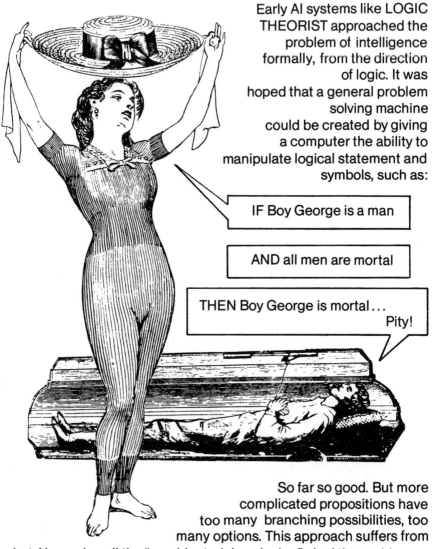

Early AI systems like LOGIC THEORIST approached the problem of intelligence formally, from the direction of logic. It was hoped that a general problem solving machine could be created by giving a computer the ability to manipulate logical statement and symbols, such as:

IF Boy George is a man

AND all men are mortal

THEN Boy George is mortal...
Pity!

So far so good. But more complicated propositions have too many branching possibilities, too many options. This approach suffers from what AI people call the "combinatorial explosion". And the problem only gets worse when you add a *knowledge base* of facts which includes all foreseeable possibilities – but no guidance about how you should go about selecting from them.

The game of chess illustrates the limitations of the formal approach. There are an estimated 10^{120} possible positions on the board. To play them all out would take billions of years. A good player limits the search for a move to the handful that promise the best lines of attack. Pure logic and even an infinite knowledge base are nothing without a system to control the decision making process.

A final problem with the formal approach is the need to represent all knowledge as numbers or logical statements – even the uncertain and often imcompatible facts and feelings found in the real world. These early programs, ambitious as they were, only used a small proportion of the intellectual powers a human being would apply to solve a problem.

So how do people think? Ironically, the search for artificial intelligence has forced both computer researchers and cognitive scientists to come to terms with this important question.

Here's why. Suppose you're living out in the middle of the Great Plains and you're supposed to attend a cable car conductors convention 1,500 miles away in San Francisco.
Unfortunately, you have no map. You begin your trip by driving down a dirt road lead to a three-way intersection. Which way do you turn?

If you choose at random, follow that route to the next intersection, choose at random again, and keep on keepin' on in the same fashion – then you just might possibly reach your destination. That is, if you have all the time and luck in the world. Unfortunately, the odds against you are estimated at 10^{30}. That's 10 followed by 30 zeros.

In a realistic situation, a person would not proceed completely at random. That's because each of us knows something about the world.

Plus we know how to ask questions about what we don't know. And we know how to solve new problems based upon what we've learned.

We know, for example, that San Francisco is to the west of us. This also happens to be the direction in which the sun sets. So we always try to choose the route that points us west. This dramatically swings the odds in our favor. And if we still get lost, a glance at a map or a kindly word with a stranger can get us back on track.

But how do you teach this kind of intelligent behavior to a machine?

Three essential skills are involved. The ability to see the world and understand what is seen. The ability to use language or pictures to communicate. And the ability to apply certain rules to solve problems. Underlying them all is the ability to learn from experience.

153

VISION

To simply hook a computer up to a video camera is not the same thing as endowing it with sight.

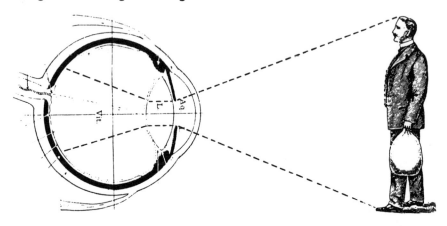

TV involves the reduction of a
3-dimensional world continuum into a flickering 2-dimensional representation that exists within a frame. Besides, *who* is in the computer watching the picture? And *who* will construct it into a model of the solid world outside?

Researcher Terry Winograd's program SHRDLU has demonstrated an ability to "see", "know", and even "move" imaginary blocks of different colors, shapes, and sizes that are displayed on screen.

If told to move one block on top of another, for instance, the computer can say whether or not it is possible (say a cube on top of a pyramid). SHRDLU can also decide which shape is behind another, which is wider or more narrow, and so on. In its own simple way, the system shows that it has learned how to operate theoretically in our 3-dimensional world.

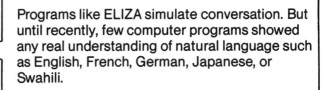

Programs like ELIZA simulate conversation. But until recently, few computer programs showed any real understanding of natural language such as English, French, German, Japanese, or Swahili.

Straight-forward text translations have produced such miracles of misunderstanding as this:

"The spirit is willing, but the flesh is weak"   rendered into

"The whiskey is fine, but the steak is not so good."

How do you teach a machine to know what words mean? You could concentrate on individual words and their meanings. But there are hundreds of thousands of words, and sometimes one word means different things in different contexts. The noun *block*, for example, and the verb to *block*.

A better way is to give the machine a sense of context along with the words. Computer scientist Roger Shank has developed the concept of "scripts", which states that human memory is organized by clusters of generalizations and expectations. And these are linked to models of the world that we carry around with us.

In a car accident script, if we say that John was hit – we can infer that he was probably hurt and possibly hospitalized.

In a restaurant script, we expect that the word "tip" means a gratuity, and not the pointed end of something.

WELL, THERE ARE TIPS AND TIPS, SIR!

Further developments in programs using "scripts theory" may result in computers that converse fairly well in a given context. But the ability to easily shift from one conversational context to another – the way people do – will probably elude machines for a long time to come.

PROBLEM SOLVING

Logic and a large memory alone are not enough to solve complicated problems. Simply playing out all possible permutations of a situation can be a waste of time, memory, and processing ability. For people and machines alike, what seems to work best is using a series of guidelines or rules of thumb to cut the problem down to size.

Heuristics is the name for these rules. Each skill and field has its own set of guidelines. They are usually obtained by studying how experts in that field solve problems. Generally, these rules can be expressed in terms of IF ... AND ... THEN.

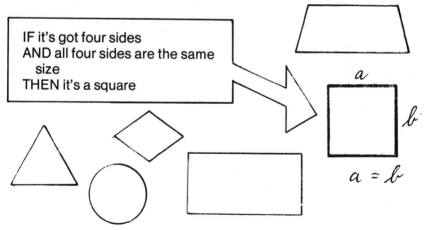

IF it's got four sides
AND all four sides are the same
    size
THEN it's a square

MYCIN, a computer program invented at Stanford to help diagnose bacterial infections of the blood, uses a *knowledge base* of 500 such rules. Like most so-called EXPERT SYSTEMS, MYCIN asks questions as it goes. If it needs more information or guidelines to diagnose a certain condition – it simply asks the user.

157

Today there are many expert software systems available for large mainframes and some of the more powerful microcomputers. Better known programs include: DENDRAL, which identifies organic molecules; CADUCEUS, which helps doctors diagnose bacterial infections; CATCH, which helps the New York City police identify suspects by scanning 250,000 photos; and PROSPECTOR, which helps pinpoint mineral deposits by evaluating geological data.

One of the reasons why expert programs seem to function intelligently is the interactive way that information flows through the system. First, a *knowledge base* is input, containing many simple facts expressed in terms of IF... THEN.

 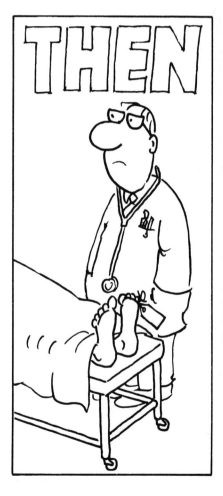

An expert medical system, for example, might contain information like:

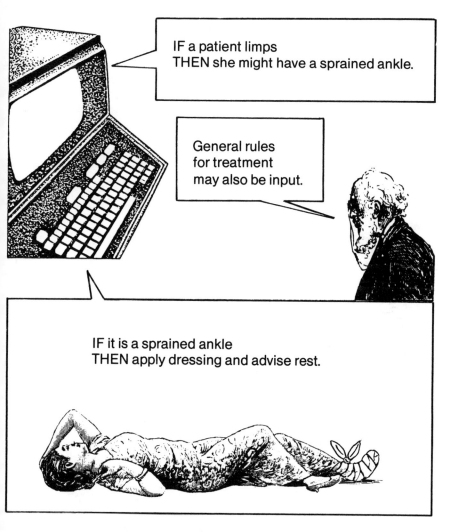

IF a patient limps
THEN she might have a sprained ankle.

General rules
for treatment
may also be input.

IF it is a sprained ankle
THEN apply dressing and advise rest.

Once the knowledge base is in place, the system is ready to deal with both the user and the problem at hand.

An *inference engine* containing a series of operational commands that links or *loops* important information through the system may now come on line. The engine is capable of inferring connections between, say, an injury, its causes, and its treatment.

Information in this system flows back and forth in a variety of directions, simulating a relatively intelligent dialog that might occur between a human expert and a non-expert.

If faced with a stubborn problem – insufficient data or guidance, for example – the operation does not simply grind to a halt. Instead the system asks further questions, draws new inferences, and comes to tentative conclusions. These are usually phrased the way a human expert might put it when she wants to hedge her bets:

My preferred therapy might be as follows...

Unlike strictly formal computer programs, expert systems are smart enough to deal with uncertainty. One business program, EXSY, lets the user assign *degrees of confidence* to possible conditions: the flip of a coin, the weather next week, the size of the soybean harvest. The certainty of possible events is expressed in numbers from 1 to 100. A coin flip, for example, might receive a value of 50, since the odds are 50:50 you'll toss a head or a tail. The computer will then rank possible outcomes according to their certainty score.

As you can see, AI increasingly relies on recognizably human patterns of thought to shape programs. Here are some of the decision-making strategies people – and computers – can use to solve problems.

REASONING BACKWARDS

This is the essence of analysis. MYCIN does this very well, in fact. It begins with a description of the patient's condition. Then it asks questions in order to narrow down the possible causes. Finally, with varying degrees of success, it makes its diagnosis.

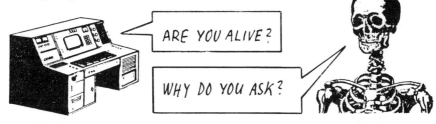

ARE YOU ALIVE?

WHY DO YOU ASK?

DIVIDE AND CONQUER

This is simply breaking complicated problems into smaller parts.

Before you'd accept a job offer, for example, you'd probably first evaluate factors such as pay, working conditions, advancement opportunities, and so on. Only then would you be in a position to intelligently weigh the pluses and minuses – and make a decision.

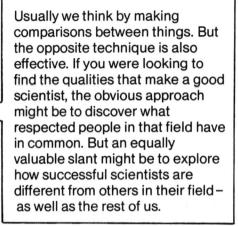

Usually we think by making comparisons between things. But the opposite technique is also effective. If you were looking to find the qualities that make a good scientist, the obvious approach might be to discover what respected people in that field have in common. But an equally valuable slant might be to explore how successful scientists are different from others in their field – as well as the rest of us.

EURISKO, a sophisticated program developed at Stanford, can do just that. Its prime function is to discover new information or rediscover information already known from basic principles. In one experiment, EURISKO was matched against human strategists in a computer war game. The object was to design a fleet of ships that could defeat the enemy in a highly-structured sea battle. Most people created armadas containing a mix of ships of different sizes.

Looking at extremes, EURISKO built a fleet around the idea of symmetry. All its ships were the same size: small and swift attack vessels much like PT boats. When the electronic dust cleared, EURISKO was the clear victor and its extreme solution was the reason.

ANALOGY

Most of us reason by comparison. When we say "Fred is like a bear," we might mean that he is big and hairy, lumbers when he walks, holes up in his apartment a lot, loves to hug, and maybe even likes honey.

Humans have many millions of memories of objects, actions, emotions, and situations on which to build just such analogies.

Computers, unfortunately, must be provided with a workable knowledge base that has plenty of facts about both our ursine friends and good ole Fred. Only then can the computer begin to make the match up.

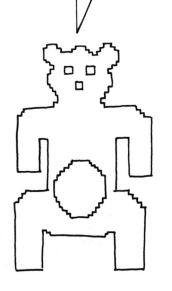

EURISKO, amazingly enough, is now able to make analogies based on its own experiences. Early in its history, the program set out to develop integrated circuit patterns for silicon chips. It came to the conclusion that a symmetrical system worked best – though it couldn't explain why. Later, when EURISKO designed its naval fleet, the computer also opted for symmetry. But this time it justified its decision by citing its earlier success with circuits. Analogy in action.

Many advanced systems are programmed to solve problems in ways that require the least amount of time and effort. Best in these circumstances might mean the simplest and most direct approach. But it could also indicate which approach seems to offer the best chances for solution. The computer decides this on the basis of past experience, as well as certain rules of thumb.

Say you wanted to know the names of all bearded American Presidents who were murdered in a theatre. The computer could search for this information under the headings of Americans, beards, murders, and theatres. Yet there have been hundreds of millions of Americans in the past centuries, doubtless tens of millions with beards, possibly a hundred thousand or so who were murdered, and certainly thousands of theatres they could've attended. Clearly, the best approach is to search under the heading of Presidents. There are only 40-something of these. Even fewer with beards.

But how does the computer know which rules of thumb are most important? Each profession has its own very specific guidelines.

Knowledge engineering is the peculiar name computer scientists have given to the exhaustive task of reducing complex areas of knowledge and skill into simple steps called *algorithms*.

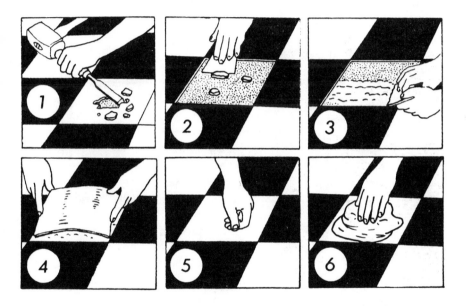

This process is actually a lot harder than it might seem, since most experts rely on intuition – not formal rules – to make decisions.

Longtime critic of AI, philosopher Hubert Dreyfus, has focused on just this problem. His studies show that human experts start out by learning rules, and then add to their knowledge by experience. Eventually, they learn to trust their educated hunches. The rules are actually forgotten. Instead experts usually refer to special cases in the past on which to base judgments.

For the skilled doctor, a certain rash combined with high fever and cramps may remind her of a case of food poisoning she treated a decade before.

For a professional driver, the car has become practically an extension of his body. He no longer has to think about the usual driving rules when he can trust his intuition.

Other critics of AI point out that while chess-playing computer programs can often beat average players, they generally fail against grandmasters. That's because human experts don't simply calculate moves. They are also able to intuitively grasp the meaning of various complicated positions on the board.

You ARE CHEATING!

Even when expert systems work – they may not work well enough to be useful. PROSPECTOR, the program that found a valuable molybdenum deposit on a mountain in Washington State, did not realize that the mineral was too deep to be worth digging. (To err is human?)

WE SHOULD HAVE STARTED DIGGING FROM CHINA!

But maybe the real secret of AI lies in hardware, not software, after all. The *architecture* of the brain is far superior to any existing computer. Although electrical signals travel much more slowly through our circuits, the elegance of our apparatus more than compensates.

We have up to 100 billion brain cells. Unlike the simple digital on/off signal, electrical impulses in our nervous system can be transmitted in a variety of different strengths. Equally important, each neuron in our brain may be connected to as many as 10,000 other neurons. The formation of connections seems to vary with different thought processes.

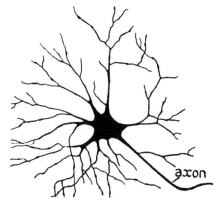

axon

167

In contrast, the typical computer based on John Von Neumann's design channels all operations through a single central processing unit. A lot of computing time is wasted going back and forth from memory to the CPU.

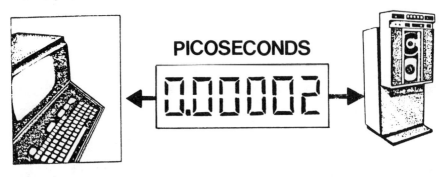

PICOSECONDS

0.00002

Our cerebral architecture allows us to work on various parts of the same – or different – problems at the same time. It also permits a richness of association duplicated by no machine...

Yet. Proposed *Fifth Generation* computers are being created with the ability to do true *parallel* processing. Imagine a machine in which thousands of tiny microprocessors are linked together to do sophisticated problems. To speed things up, memory and processing ability are distributed throughout the system — much like in the human brain. American and Japanese developers are feverishly pursuing this "Non Von" solution to AI.

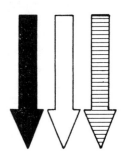

But even if we can do it, why should we want to create an intelligent machine? Curiosity is one reason. What would silicon-based intelligence be like? Would it differ from our own? Could it supply answers to some of the great questions we've struggled for millennia to answer?

Another reason sees intelligent computers as possible earth emissaries to the stars, sent into space on century-long voyages.

HI ! TAKE ME TO YOUR LEADER!

A third reason is that discoveries in the AI field may tell us a lot about the function of our own intelligence – much the way that studying bird flight not only tell us about birds, but also about principles of aerodynamics we can use to build planes.

A final reason is that as our world becomes more complicated, intelligent machines may be able to help us run it better. Humans have infinite processing power but limited memory; computers have infinitely-extendable memory but only limited processing power. How about a partnership?

As computers become more intelligent, it will become easier for people to enlist their assistance and memory. *Voice-recognition* capacity may soon give us the ability to ask for detailed information and get it instantly. Sophisticated information processing systems may be able to cull through data, eliminate 99% of the less promising information, and draw our attention to the 1% that matters.

Advanced decision-making systems may be able to help people solve problems more rationally, more quickly, and with a better chance of success.

And one day Hyper-Intelligent Machines may be able to pass the toughest test of all and become...

Good company, interesting- enough in their own right to find a valued place in our journey through life.

Chapter VIII
FINAL SILICONSIDERATIONS

*"I never think about the future.
It comes soon enough."*
— Albert Einstein

Synergy is the idea that the combined action of a whole is greater than the sum of its parts. The use of computers in all areas of science and society is clearly having a synergistic effect on progress – speeding up many developments and bringing the future to us all that much sooner.

Unlike Einstein, many of us do think about the future. Naturally, we want to plan ahead far enough in our own lives so as not to get left behind.

But sometimes we can also let our anticipations get the better of us.

Our society has long believed in the myth that technical solutions will cure all woes. For some of us, computers have turned this myth into mania.

We fear that without high tech in our lives the future is bleak. Our small store front business will fail.

Worse, our kids will become deprived, sub-technological savages.

Our homes will cease to function. We won't even be able to balance our checkbook.

The fact is that computers are not for everyone – in every situation.

Consider the rush to place computers in the schools. When teachers have been trained to use them, when there are enough machines to go around, and when each kid can actually play around with the system for at least a few hours a week – then students seem to benefit. Visual and creative skills may actually improve, especially in areas like art, geometry, and writing composition.

Yet an important New England study showed no advantage in using computers to teach basic skills. Inexpensive workbooks and flash cards seemed to teach reading and writing as well or better than expensive machines. Perhaps putting money in trained teachers is a much more cost-effective solution.

But how about helping children to become more *computer literate*? This too may be a self-deception.

When today's elementary school student will be applying for a job, computers will probably be more *user-friendly* than today. Maybe they'll even be able to respond to voice commands. Rather than teaching specific computer skills, doesn't it make more sense to teach kids how to think and learn on their own? In this way, they'll be prepared regardless of the changes the future will bring.

Resourcefulness and flexibility in the face of change is also the key to success in the work world. Each year 100,000 new computer programmers graduate from community colleges in the US. But unless these people constantly upgrade their skills – in a sense, learn how to learn – they too may become obsolete, under-skilled, and unemployed. New technologies quickly make existing systems ancient history. Worse, the need for programmers to design customized programs may shrink as more inexpensive commercially-produced software packages come onto the market.

There simply is no substitute for being able to think clearly. Yet many individuals and companies invest in expensive hardware without giving a thought about how they want to use it. Does a person really need a home computer to store phone numbers and dinner recipes, or to help fill out a tax form?

Should a company install a new electronic filing system without training staff to use it?

How can all of us begin to learn that no technological innovation can solve our problems by itself. The human mind is still the best problem solver of all.

Yet the computer is clearly here to stay. Productivity aside, we as a species seem to like this new breed of machine. Perhaps our race has always tended to see the human in all things. In mythic times, we endowed trees, rivers, and even the stars with names and personalities.

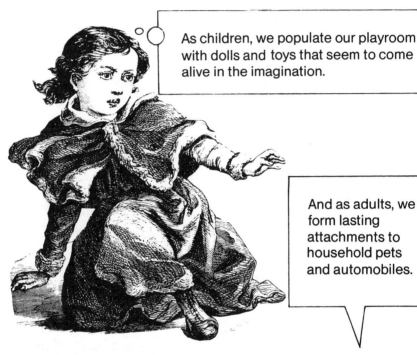

As children, we populate our playroom with dolls and toys that seem to come alive in the imagination.

And as adults, we form lasting attachments to household pets and automobiles.

Intelligent machines seem to be even more seductive. Joseph Weizenbaum, creator of pseudo-therapist ELIZA, recalls:

"People who knew very well that they were conversing with a machine soon forgot that fact... They would demand to be permitted to converse with the system in private and would, after conversing with it for a little time, insist, in spite of my explanations, that the machine really understood them."

176

Sometimes knowing that a program like ELIZA was totally computerized actually increased its effectiveness. People seemed to feel that a machine would be more impartial and less judgmental.

Several patients who had recently lost someone close to them confided in the machine, but not in a human counselor. In an English study, alcoholics confessed to the computer that they actually drank considerably more than they were willing to admit to another person.

Will we one day also have vinyl vicars, plastic pastors, and electronic rabbis to tell our troubles to?

Computers are having other unsettling effects on human relations. In recent years, an increasing number of people have discovered that getting along well with a machine sometimes makes it harder to get close to another individual. Consider the compulsive hacker, an infomaniac with eyes bugged-out from too much monitor watching, surviving on junk food and soft drinks, seldom sleeping, punching keys until he drops, and *grokking* technospeak better than any human tongue.

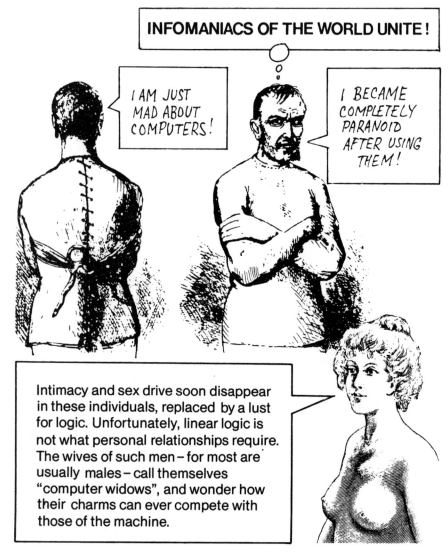

INFOMANIACS OF THE WORLD UNITE!

I AM JUST MAD ABOUT COMPUTERS!

I BECAME COMPLETELY PARANOID AFTER USING THEM!

Intimacy and sex drive soon disappear in these individuals, replaced by a lust for logic. Unfortunately, linear logic is not what personal relationships require. The wives of such men – for most are usually males – call themselves "computer widows", and wonder how their charms can ever compete with those of the machine.

Will computers force us to think about human beings in a new way? Remember the anger and shock that most people felt when Charles Darwin claimed that we were not descended from Adam – but from the apes. It took a long while before we got comfortable with the idea of people as intelligent animals.

Will we ever get used to the idea that we are emotional machines?

What, after all, is the future of the human:computer connection?

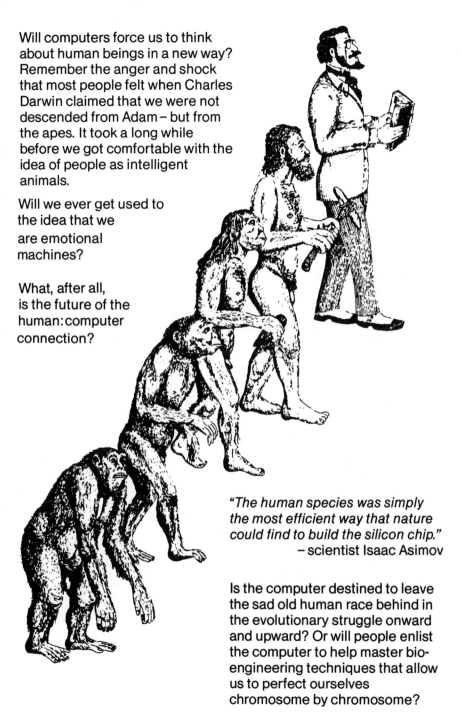

"The human species was simply the most efficient way that nature could find to build the silicon chip."
– scientist Isaac Asimov

Is the computer destined to leave the sad old human race behind in the evolutionary struggle onward and upward? Or will people enlist the computer to help master bio-engineering techniques that allow us to perfect ourselves chromosome by chromosome?

Will we grow weak, lazy, and hopelessly decadent, with nothing to do but amuse ourselves relentlessly any way we can?

Will we be able to harness the machine to develop godlike mental powers, enabling us to literally convert wish into deed, mind into matter? Will we also be able to tame our destructive impulses as we make the transition from ape into angel?

Will the machines eventually get the upper hand, and force us to conform to their reign of reason and regimentation? Who is destined to rule whom?

Or will the machines finally tire of our foibles and failings, and make an end to the human experiment once and for all?

These are only a handful of the conceivable futures ahead of us. A good thing to keep in mind is that as much as we need the computer, it needs us even more. Humans not only created the machine, we provide it with a purpose, a reason for being.

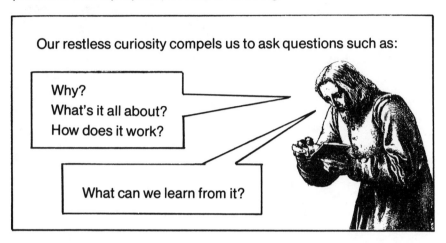

Our restless curiosity compels us to ask questions such as:

Why?
What's it all about?
How does it work?

What can we learn from it?

We have no choice but to ask these and other questions. It's our nature. The mission of the computer is to help us discover the answers that lead us to the next frontier of knowledge – and beyond.

And who could want a better basis for a lasting partnership?

BIBLIOGRAPHY

BIT BY BIT: AN ILLUSTRATED HISTORY OF COMPUTERS, by Stan Augarten. Unwin Paperbacks, London, Boston & Sydney. 1985.

THE COMPUTER FROM PASCAL TO VON NEUMANN, by Herman H. Goldstine. Princeton University Press, Princeton, N. J. 1980.

ELECTRONIC INVENTIONS AND DISCOVERIES, by G. W. A. Dummer. 3rd Edition. Pergamon Press, Oxford. 1983.

THE ELECTRONIC COTTAGE: EVERYDAY LIVING WITH YOUR PERSONAL COMPUTERS, by Joseph Deken. Bantam Books, Toronto & London. 1981.

ENGINES OF THE MIND: A HISTORY OF THE COMPUTER, by Joel Shurkin. W. W. Norton & Company, New York & London. 1984.

AN INTRODUCTION TO MICROCOMPUTERS: THE BEGINNER'S BOOK, by Adam Osborne & David Bunnell. 3rd Edition. McGraw-Hill, Inc., New York. 1982.

MATHEMATICAL THOUGHT FROM ANCIENT TO MODERN TIMES, by Morris Kline. Oxford University Press, Oxford. 1972.

THE MAKING OF THE MICRO: A HISTORY OF THE COMPUTER, by Christopher Evans. Gollancz. London. 1981/Van Nostrand Reinhold, New York. 1981.

THE MICRO MILLENIUM, by Christopher Evans. Viking Press. New York. 1980.

MICROPROCESSORS: A STEP-BY-STEP INTRODUCTION. Spectrum Books. Prentice Hall International, Englewood Cliffs, N. J. & London.

THE MIGHTY MICRO, by Christopher Evans. Gollancz. London. 1979/Van Nostrand Reinhold, New York. 1981.

THE RANDOM HOUSE BOOK OF COMPUTER LITERACY, by Ellen Richman. Vintage Books, New York. 1983.

COMPUTERS: THE NEXT GENERATION (Tomorrow's world series), by Jack Weber. Arco Publishing, Inc., New York. 1985/British Broadcasting Corporation, London. 1984.

WITHOUT ME YOU'RE NOTHING: THE ESSENTIAL GUIDE TO HOME COMPUTERS, by Frank Herbert with Max Barnard. Simon & Schuster, New York. 1981/Gollancz, London. 1981.

INDEX

Picture credits
Cray 1 – supercomputer – courtesy of Cray Research; Napier's Bones, Pascal's calculator – courtesy of Harrow House Editions Ltd.; Blaise Pascal, Charles Babbage – photo Science Museum; Babbage's Analytical Engine, Herman Hollerith, Hollerith's tabulator, IBM logo, Mark 1 – courtesy of IBM; Alan Turing – courtesy of Heffer & Sons Ltd.; ENIAC, UNIVAC – courtesy of Sperry Ltd.; Kilby's integrated circuit – courtesy of Texas Instruments Incorporated; Noyce's integrated circuit – courtesy of Intel Corporation (U.K.) Ltd.; Ferranti F 100-L Chip – courtesy of Ferranti Computer Systems Ltd. Thanks to Dover Publications, NY for their permission to use Harter's Picture Archive for Collage edited by Jim Harter.